Parenting Apprenticeship

Nurturing Teenagers Through a New Lens

by
Eunice Essien

**Kingdom
Publishers**

Parenting Apprenticeship

Nurturing Teenagers Through a New Lens

Copyright© Eunice Essien

A catalogue record for this book is available from the British Library.

All Scripture Quotations have been taken from the New King James Version Life Application Study Bible.

ISBN: 978-1-911697-34-3

1st Edition by Kingdom Publishers

Kingdom Publishers
London, UK.

You can purchase copies of this book from any leading bookstore or email

contact@kingdompublishers.co.uk

Dedication

To my beautiful children, Monique and Myron from whom I have learned so much, that you will grow to become committed parenting apprentices.

To my sisters, Gladys and Sarah; to the Essiens and the Yambilas for your support that make me feel the arms of God around me.

To my brother Sampson, I am grateful.

To my brother Pastor John for your relentless prayers and encouragement.

To the mothers and fathers of Love (**www.essiens.org**) that the nurturing of your children may bring you peace and fulfilment.

To all parents and everyone caring for children, that you may rediscover parenthood as it was intended to be.

"And the Lord, He is the One that goes before you. He will be with you; He will never leave you nor forsake you; do not fear or be dismayed." – Deuteronomy 31:8

Parenting Apprenticeship
Nurturing Teenagers Through a New Lens

Contents

FIRST THINGS FIRST

'There are many plans in a man's heart, nevertheless the Lord's counsel – that will stand.' – Proverbs 19:21

Chapter 1

Meet the Parenting Apprentice

First, allow me to tell you who and what I am not. I am not a scientist nor a professor of any kind. I am not a doctor, a lawyer nor a clinical psychologist. I am not here in a capacity of any profession although I have been trained to Masters' level with a qualification as a Paediatric Nurse and Specialist Community Public Health Nurse (Health Visitor).

Now allow me to share with you who I am. My name is Eunice and I am fearfully and wonderfully made in God's image. I was born in the late 70s and grew up in Ghana, West Africa. I am the ninth born of ten children. Yes! A big family, I know. I moved to the United Kingdom nearly 20 years ago. I am here to share my story with you. I am a mother blessed with two wonderful teenagers: my daughter is 19 years and my son is 13 years old. I am a committed parenting apprentice. I am a woman who has experienced marriage and also divorce. I am a woman who has become intentional in her life as a result of my hunger for change and growth, and who has discovered truths in the process. I am a woman who has found her identity and has been enlightened to operate from that identity: a formidable, tried and tested foundation. I am a woman whose purpose is to share my story with you to empower, challenge and yet invigorate you. I share my story as a mother.

'For lack of knowledge my people perish' – Hosea 4:6

Allow me to draw your attention to something that I have observed. When I look around me, I see that the divorce rate is high. The rate at which relationships are breaking down is alarming. And when I asked the question why is this happening? I have come to one important conclusion: ignorance! Many of us are behaving foolishly because we as a people lack the knowledge of the principles of relationships and marriage. Please do not be offended. This is not to insult anyone, but the behaviour of many of us is foolish. In fact, we are not interested in the truth and so we reject the truth. The truth is the truth. It does not matter whether I like it or not, it is the truth. It does not matter whether I believe it or not, it is the truth. The truth remains the truth regardless of my acceptance of it or my belief. The truth does not change because I feel uncomfortable. For many of us, no one has actually taught us the foundations and principles of marriage and so we do not know what to expect. There are others who know but also choose to behave ignorantly and so we are perishing in our relationships. It is not enough just to know; it is about knowing but also about doing – that is where growth comes in. Experience can exist without growth, so can knowledge. And until we learn and grow ourselves as men and women and in the principles of the institution; many of us will continue to enter into unfulfilling relationship after unfulfilling relationship, marriage after marriage which may lead to heartbreaks and divorce. You may be wondering by now why am I talking about marriage and relationships when the title of this book is *Parenting Apprenticeship*? Here is why.

I have observed that in our world today many maturing adults, young people, teenagers and adult children are 'divorcing' their parents. Yes 'divorcing' their parents! Of course, not in the same sense as marriage relationships but the basis is the same because they are lack the knowledge, understanding and wisdom of the principles of relationships. The relationships between parents and their adult children are estranged. There are parents who disown their teenagers or adult children and there are teenagers and adult children who do not want anything to do with their parents. As I share with you now, the relationship between my daughter and her father is estranged. It has been broken down since September, 2018. The relationship became difficult when my daughter was approaching her adolescent years, it continued to get worse until the relationship broke down when my daughter turned 17. I must say that the relationship between my daughter and I at the time was not good either, but it was better than the one between her and her father. She had lost trust for me as her mother and I think that she had felt unloved. I have had to work hard to rebuild the trust between my daughter and I. I continue to be intentional to maintain her trust and to continue the flourishing relationship we have now.

I think that society is experiencing estranged relationships between parents and their children at a high rate. The relationship between parents and their maturing adults are increasingly becoming unfulfilling and hence the estrangement or 'divorce' so to speak that later ensues. Apart from my own experience, I know parents whose adult children have 'divorced' them and I also know others that are on verge of being 'divorced'. As you read my story now, you may be experiencing such estrangement in your own relationship with your teenagers or adult children. My heart goes out to you all. My heart goes out to the young people and the adult children as well. Take it from someone who understands and knows because I have experienced such estrangement. I must admit that there may be differences in the complexities and specifics of details but I believe the basis remains the same. Many a time estranged relationships may seem farther away from you than you might think, but for some it can be closer than you think.

Our world is complicated now more than ever. It is not as simple as it used to be. Our world is getting complex each day, each month and each year. We have a lot of conveniences yet less time. I have realised that we have easy access to information yet we lack understanding and wisdom in a lot of things. I think the sad thing is that many people do not even comprehend this, let alone admit to not knowing: ignorance. With these complexities come the complexities in our relationships too. We are failing in our relationships too because we lack the understanding and the wisdom to relate to our children and teenagers. I have come to refer to parenting as nurturing as I have grown from taking my parenting apprenticeship seriously. I will explain to you why I have arrived at such a conclusion in due course.

Just as many of us are oblivious to the principles of relationships and marriage, so are we ignorant of the principles of nurturing our children too. I was no exception. For the first 15 years of being a mother and a parent, I parented anyhow. I became a mother in 2001. It was a couple of weeks before my 24th birthday. I parented like everyone else around me. I practised what I have come to call 'leave-it-to-chance parenting' or 'everyday parenting'. But now that I have been enlightened; I am blessed to say that I see things differently. I have a new perspective, a change of perspective that makes things purposeful, meaningful and fulfilling. I have only arrived here from where I have journeyed from because I made the decision to take my parenting apprenticeship seriously. It is this journey I share with you in this book. I will discuss some of the modules and lessons I have been blessed with here in this book with you. I pray that as you read and journey on with me, you will be challenged and yet empowered to take your own journey of parenting apprenticeship seriously in order to bring meaning and fulfilment to your life and your teenagers' lives.

Parenting Apprenticeship focuses on the nurturing of our children and teenagers as parents. I have written this book from the experience and perspective of my life as a woman and as a mother. It is my personal story of experience, knowledge, understanding and growth in my journey of being a parent. I have used the concept of apprenticeship to capture the essence of the 'job description' of parenting. Not only is it an apprenticeship, it is also a career that develops and grows over time. It is a journey over a parent's life time because as a parent, you never stop being a parent just because your children become adults or you become 'divorced' by your children. It is a career that once you take it seriously and embark on it, you cannot decide one day to say that "I am going to have a career change or I don't want to be a parent any longer." No! I must however, admit that some parents sadly choose to be irresponsible and abandon their parenting apprenticeship career along the way. It is sad that it happens, but that is the reality sometimes. Having said that, the truth remains, it does not change the fact that they are parents.

I have not always seen parenting as an apprenticeship career, not until late 2016. I am not saying that I abandoned my role as a mother, what I am saying is that I did not view it through the lens of an apprenticeship let alone a career. Chapters 2 and 3 of this book shed some light on my parenting prior to viewing parenting from the lens of an apprenticeship, and the results or fruits thereof to give you a better understanding. As you continue to read and journey with me, you will realise that I am using nurturing more and more. In fact, I have come to view nurturing as having a deeper meaning and the more I have reflected on the word I have gained deeper understanding as a mother. I attribute this to taking my apprenticeship seriously.

Let me explore with you why I consider parenting as an apprenticeship. Tell me, did you receive training or qualification before you became a parent; well apart from having sex and becoming pregnant and choosing to carry the pregnancy to term? Well, I did not and if I am guessing correctly no one does. You learn on the job, am I right? That is apprenticeship. Of course, without the money. Let me ask, is apprenticeship a career? Yes, I would say. So, if parenting is an apprenticeship because you learn on the job, then I am right to say that it is a career, although parents don't get the monetary reward. It is a job that we go in with no formal education or experience and it is full-time 24 hours a day lasting a lifetime, with no monetary rewards. Very interesting I would say! However, if the parenting apprenticeship is delivered diligently and purposefully, it is very rewarding, fulfilling and the job satisfaction is excellent.

When I was in a full-time education or 9-5 job and I was also in the parenting apprenticeship (automatically enrolled for becoming a mother), it meant that I was working two careers. Oh, don't get me wrong, I was aware that I was working two jobs, however what I did not comprehend fully was the implications of having two full-time careers. What happened was, I excelled at my 9-5 job whilst my parenting career was left to chance because I was doing 'everyday parenting'. Everyday parenting to me is not being intentional about nurturing. There was no way I could work both careers with the same level of attention to detail. One had to give! I am not implying that as mothers we don't have to work to pay the bills; what I am saying is that not only would we be burnt out, but the reality is that, one would take priority over the other. It is essential that you know what your priorities are and decide what is more important for you and your family.

So, meet the parenting apprentice!

'Every good and perfect gift is from above, and comes down from the father of lights, with whom there is no variation or shadow of turning.' – James 1:17

Chapter 2

Making sense of the situation

I had my first child when I was 24 years old. So, I was not a teenager but I was pretty young. I would like to say that my life circumstance was difficult and tough at the time. I mean, I was about to start my final year at university when I fell pregnant. I had come to London from Ghana, for a student work-abroad programme and this happened. So of course, you can imagine the disappointment from family and people around me. I was disappointed in myself too because I did not plan to get myself pregnant. In fact, that was not on my plans any time soon – at the time. However how naïve; what did I expect when I decided to have unprotected sex. Can I say I did not think it would happen? I have come to believe that it was meant to happen and I also believed that there was a reason why it happened, because it was out of character for me. I thought of myself as a decent woman and I still do. Oh well... I was however determined to rise above the disappointment and embarrassment and make the most of my life for myself and my unborn baby.

I thought at the time that bringing up a baby, was not an issue. I had it in the bag. How hard could this be? How could setting boundaries and managing behaviour be hard? How could making baby faces and speaking baby language be anything difficult? How could changing baby nappies be difficult? I thought I had it all covered and figured out. Well, it better be, because I was already pregnant and there was no going back from that for me.

I had bigger fish to fry. When I say bigger fish to fry, I was referring to developing a career to create the financial stability for my baby. I thought at the time that the financial responsibility was priority. You know, many people think about the affordability as soon as they think about someone who is pregnant or planning a baby. I was not thinking about parenting apprenticeship or being a committed apprentice: I had no concept of that. I was thinking about a career that rewarded me with money. That's right! I wanted to return to university to study, to build a career to provide for my daughter. I wanted the best for my child and I was determined to work hard to provide that for my daughter. That was a good thing. For me to be able to do that I had to go back into formal education. I was studying Banking and Finance at the University of Ghana and I had just completed my third year when I found myself pregnant. I had to forfeit my fourth year which was also my final year. A year after the birth of my daughter, well a couple of months before my daughter's first birthday, I was married to her father in April 2002. My life had moved so fast from going into my last year of university education, to being in a foreign land to having a baby and now married. I was married a few months before my 25th birthday in 2002. Looking at my age, I mean 25 years, it is thought to be an okay age to be married; however, marriage I have come to learn is not just about being old enough or being at a right age.

Fast forward! My daughter started full time school aged 3 years and 3 months. This was perfect time for me to get back into education. I changed my course of study when I could not gain admission to the university. I had applied to study Banking and Finance in London. I made another application to a different university where I developed a career in Child Health Nursing. I juggled parenting, going back to university education and juggling my career. I succeeded in my education and my career as I became a paediatric nurse in 2007, then a Specialist Community Public Health Nurse (Health Visitor) in 2012 and then went on to obtain my Masters' degree in Public Health in 2015. From 2004 to 2018 I had been in education or full-time employment, and sometimes a combination of both, apart from taking a year out when I was blessed with my son in October, 2007.

The 'alien'

It got to a time when my daughter was approaching adolescence that 'everyday parenting' had become an unbearable task. Shouting, arguments, resistance, rebellion and my daughter would not respond to what I call 'everyday parenting' that I had used for years without even thinking about it. Strategies including behaviour management that I had learnt from my parents or observed from others and used to parent my children without even realising it were not working any longer. It got to a time when my daughter 'shut down' and would not talk about her feelings or express herself when I genuinely wanted to know. I was unsure how to get through to her. Consequently, I demanded for her to speak, but the more I demanded the silence intensified. My daughter, my son, my husband (now my ex-husband) and I had all become unhappy in the household. My daughter's friends had stopped coming around to our home; she stopped doing the daily household responsibilities that she used to do. She looked unhappy, depressed and spent long hours in her room. She was not a big eater anyways but she would skip meals sometimes.

Both her father and I could not get through to her. She was on the verge of 'I don't care' and she used to say that quite a lot. No matter what you said to her, she responded with 'I don't care' – if we were lucky. Oh, am I kidding myself, thinking she was on the verge of not caring? She actually did not care whatever happened to her life, at least that was how I interpreted it at the time. I wondered, where was my adorable little girl? Who was this imposter! Little did I know that all the years of criticism; the attitude of 'I am the adult and you are the child' from her father and I; and 'everyday parenting' have created this 'alien'. We were not irresponsible parents; we did not know how to parent the right way. We did not know the truth about nurturing.

It was just too much, just too exhausting, just too demanding and unfulfilling; battling in the home environment. I remember that there was a day that I actually called the police to come and remove my daughter from my home following an argument. I did not know what to do. It was that bad. I felt that she was disrespectful, ungrateful and utterly rude. Guess what the police did? They did not come of course!

They redirected me to call the social services. I felt so stupid when I hung up. I felt helpless and confused. But then I thought to myself if I couldn't parent my own child, who do I think could?

The last straw was when I called her one day to help me to the bathroom because I was unwell. She blatantly refused and said, "No!" I had called her father first but he had ignored me because he was upset with me with something I couldn't remember. In the past my daughter would help me when I found myself in similar situations. That was one of my wake-up calls. My stomach churned and I felt sick to my stomach. I felt something was seriously wrong. I needed to do something different with my parenting. This was not right and I would certainly not accept this as normal. Believe me it is easy to begin to normalise situations or behaviours just because enough people are experiencing similar occurrences. Many parents think that because their teenagers or maturing adults are behaving in a certain manner, then it is normal. There are behaviours expected of teenagers because they are teenagers and there are others that are not 'normal' teenage behaviours. I don't know about you but I was not accepting this as 'normal'.

My daughter was in her mid-teenage years by now and I was thinking to myself, her younger brother was also approaching double figures in age. What would he also be doing? I had to take a serious look at my parenting and evaluate. From where I was standing, it was not looking good from the fruits I was seeing from my children.

Changing gear

So, as you can see and imagine, I had been struggling with relationships at home. The relationship between my husband and I was difficult and the relationship between my daughter and I also required attention. And the relationship between my daughter and her father was even worse. My son was feeling the impact of the unhealthy relationships. So, I had decided to do things differently and I was learning and researching in that manner. I wanted to be a better mother to my teenagers because I realised that if I did not, I would lose them. Things were that bad. There were arguments between my husband and I and there was also tension between my husband and our daughter which I was drawn into as well. It was chaos and misery. I could feel the negative energy. It was palpable. It felt thick and so heavy in the air and sometimes suffocating to the lungs. Sometimes the silence treatment in the house was deafening. The stress levels were sky-high.

Talking about stress: remember I said my daughter became withdrawn and isolated herself in her room. She had also gone into the 'I don't care mode'. My daughter said at one point that if it was not because of her little brother, she would have left home. I remember when she managed to secure a job when she was 16yrs of age in 2017, guess who was her next of kin? Her 9-year-old younger brother. That was how much she had lost trust in her father and I, her parents.

My son was younger; he was overwhelmed and sometimes confused so, he would cry whenever there were arguments and he seemed miserable. My husband was upset, stressed, angry and in my opinion depressed too. I on the other hand, in 2017, was diagnosed with vitiligo localised to my lips. Vitiligo is a long-term condition where white patches develop on the skin. It is caused by the lack of melanin, which is the pigment in the skin. I remember the doctor asking me whether there was any genetic disposition of this condition, for which the answer was: "Not to the best of my knowledge." The dermatologist asked whether I was stressed as the condition can be stressed-induced or activated especially considering the fact that I did not have a genetic disposition. I was like: "No! me? No stress at all." I knew that things were stressful but I did not think that it would affect me in that way because I believed I was a tough cookie. Here I was denying stress when everything about me at the time was screaming, "stressed!" On top of the diagnosis of vitiligo, I had lost so much weight, my once tight and hugging pair of jeans were now hanging loose on my legs. To make matters worse, my skin was breaking out with acne and spots. My face beaded with spots and acne – never in my life had I experienced so much acne. And yet I said I was not stressed. I was not sure what that was about. I was not sure whether I could not see that as stress, or whether I was in denial or a combination of both at the time. I could tell from a mile when others were stressed but I could not admit to myself that I was stressed. Now sharing and talking about it, it goes to show how easy it is to point out issues in others rather than in ourselves. So, my home environment was far from nurturing and no one was happy.

In the midst of all this, I uncovered something very important. I uncovered that in my professional work as a health visitor and children's nurse, I supported families to deal with these kinds of tension in their relationships at home. I worked collaboratively with other professionals to come out with strategies to support families in a similar situation to my own family. Then, it hit me. My question to myself at the time was: "What am I doing?" I worked with families to implement strategies to better the relationships within the home to support the health and emotional wellbeing of their children. Who was I to go out to do that when I couldn't quench the fire in my own home? What sort of hypocritical life was I living? I covered up what was happening in my own life and had the audacity to go and carry out assessments of families in a similar situation? Things were rotten in my own home; however, I went round pointing the rottenness in other people's lives. What was worse, I was paid for doing that because I was acting in my professional role. Oh my God, how hypocritical; double standards. Who am I? What is this? What happened to me? I felt sick to my stomach yet again when I realised that I was leading such a double life.

Sometimes we normalise and rationalise the things happening in our own lives and yet we point our fingers at others. Sometimes we may say, "My situation is better than hers or his or theirs." At the end of the day, it is not about comparison with others. It is about becoming the best person we can be and leading our best lives. We are in competition with ourselves to develop and grow into our fullest potential. I came to the conclusion that something needed to change. I had to change. I didn't want to be that person. I resolved that in order to be effective in supporting parents and families outside, I had to put my home in order, I had to put myself in order. Isn't that what 'charity begins at home' is all about? I started to make some changes but it was so tough and difficult. I later realised that it was so unbearable and tedious because I was doing things based on my own strength. I had no support, no back-up, no foundation, so I felt the whole strain. Things were bad, I will share more details as we journey along.

I started research and reading. The resources I was using for my research and learning has references from scripture. Some way somehow, I started to read my bible and started to pray. I had also watched the movie, *War Room*. It was about a woman whose marriage was in turmoil and the relationship with her daughter required attention too. She was taught by an older woman to overcome her problems by strategically battling spiritually through prayer. She dedicated her closet for prayers. In essence her closet became her battlefield. Spiritual battlefield. You wouldn't believe it but, I built myself a war room in my cupboard. I did not have a closet so I made use of the next best thing available to me. That was a cupboard in my bedroom. I used to store my dirty laundry basket in that cupboard. I prepared the cupboard and it became functional, fit for purpose. As nurses would say, "Fit for practice". It was after I drew closer to God and decided to spend time in His presence that I realised the connectivity, the connection. Things took on a new turn. Oh, don't get me wrong, things were still tough but I felt less stressed. I did not feel the pressure as much. I could not explain it, but it was the truth.

As time went on, I discovered my identity in the process which gave me grounding. My identity is in God and it became clearer through His word. This was where my foundation became visible to me in the sense that I found that my foundation is based on my relationship with God. I concluded that my foundation is my walk with God. From my foundation I drew on other priorities that were important to me such as being a nurturing and loving mother and wife. Once I was able to determine my foundation, I lived from it; that is, operating from my foundation. My priorities changed; I set new ones, made some amendments to some values and reaffirmed others, I set new standards and morals. I was on a mission and I was determined; I had direction; I had focus. I became intentional and purposeful in the things I did. That was when I was enlightened to view parenting through the lens of apprenticeship, which I will throw light on in the chapters to come.

I am not going to pretend that this process was easy or has been easy because it has not. Author, Van Moody likens the process of self-discovery to the process of peeling an onion in his book, *The I factor: How Building a Great Relationship with Yourself is the Key to a Happy Successful Life*. I learned that it is important to get back to the core in order to be able to live from the healthy place of my true identity. To be able to do this I had to strip away who I was not, that is, all the layers that I had piled on top of me over time. I had to do this layer by layer just like peeling an onion. We all know that process can sting your eyes and make your kitchen and your fingers stink, and sometimes your eyes water as if you are crying and feel pain. Sometimes we step away, wipe our tears and then continue. My eyes flooded with tears, my fingers stunk and I even cut my finger sometimes but I wiped my tears and washed the blood off my fingers, dressed my finger and continued the peeling.

Although it is not an easy process, I do know that it is worthwhile. I will do the whole process again if I had to because the fruits are delicious, scrumptious and fulfilling. I feel good in myself now. I enjoy this inner peace and joy due to the growth in myself from the changes I have made, and the relationship I enjoy with my teenagers now is priceless. From "I hate you; I don't care; you stress me out" to "I love you; you are my best friend." These were statements from my daughter. I can also see the ripple effect on my relationship with others.

So far, I have given you a taster of where I have come from, some of the fruits of where I was when I was parenting 'anyhow'. For example, I had excelled at my academic studies and career and failed miserably at parenting. I did not realise that this was going to happen until my daughter was approaching adolescence; until I was presented with an 'alien'. I have also shared with you some of the instances that necessitated the move towards change and growth for me. This move and growth gave birth to *Parenting Apprenticeship*. The coming chapters will throw light on parenting apprenticeship: what it means and what it involves as I continue to share my story.

*'I will praise You for I am fearfully and wonderfully made…
and that my soul knows very well.'- Psalm 139:14*

Chapter 3

Who are you learning from?

I ask the question, "who am I learning from?" I have come to the conclusion that parenting is an apprenticeship because we as parents learn on the job, with no prior experience or training. So, my question to you today is, "Who are you learning from?" What is more? With every child, you require a different set of strategies and skills because each child is different. This is one of the reasons why I have come to prefer the word 'nurturing' to parenting. As I am hoping that you do agree with me that parenting is an apprenticeship, then stay with me. In the realm of apprenticeship, the apprentice has someone that he or she learns from, someone that supervises and teaches him or her. Someone who handles things that the apprentice is not yet capable of handling. Someone who answers the apprentice's questions and concerns. Someone who disciplines and gives constructive feedback to the apprentice. Someone who commends and encourages the apprentice on a good job done. Someone the apprentice looks up to. So, my question to you is:

- Who are you learning from as an apprentice?
- Who is supervising you in your career as a nurturing apprentice?
- Who is the manager you look up to?
- Who is teaching you how to nurture your teenagers?
- Who is guiding you?
- Who encourages you when you are low on strength?
- When things become tough, and they do, who do you turn to for help? Society, social media, peers who are also struggling; who?
- Who are you learning from?

I hope you get where I am coming from and what I am driving at. As soon as I was enlightened to view nurturing of my teenagers as an apprenticeship, I was also enlightened to some truths. With these truths came certain principles and understanding. I am glad and blessed for the opportunity to share this with you. I hope that these truths will be meaningful and would inform your nurturing as much as they have mine in your journeys of parenting apprenticeship.

I was enlightened to some truths as I mentioned:

'Children are a heritage from the Lord, the fruit of the womb is a reward.' - Psalm 127:3

My children are gifts from God and they are also a heritage from God. I was enlightened to what it meant for my children to be a gift from God and a heritage from God at the same time. It means that my children, ultimately belong to Him who gave them to me because I am accountable to Him. I came to the understanding that I am but a steward, or if you like a caretaker with no experience. Hence, I have to recognise and allow God to nurture my children through me. So, what I am saying is that God nurtures my children through me. Another truth I learned was the fact that I have been given the opportunity to be a mother and parent not because I deserved it, but for a purpose. Now, this was a revelation! What is this purpose? How was I to know the purpose when I was oblivious to the fact that my children are a heritage from the Lord?

And for 15 years I did not know this truth and the principles thereof. So, I took things in my own hands and parented 'anyhow'. I did not recognise let alone allow Him, who gave me my children to show me, to teach me, to direct me and to supervise me. Talk about allowing Him to parent through me was beyond me. I leaned on my own understanding to parent my children and I did what I thought was my best but the fact was I had strayed and gone off tangent for 15 years. The result was not encouraging. I got my priorities wrong because I did my own thing. I did things like everyone else or most people. I followed the crowd blindly. Scripture says:

'Trust in the Lord your God with all your heart, and lean not on your own understanding, in all things acknowledge him and he will direct your path.' – Proverbs 3:5-6.

Here I was employed as an apprentice for a purpose and I was ignorant of that truth. Many parents parent the same way that I did and the results are not favourable. I think that as a result of taking things into our own hands we unknowingly sometimes steer our children into 'divorcing' us or living unfulfilling and miserable lives even though they may be making loads and loads of money in their adult lives. As I mentioned earlier, there are many parents out there whose maturing adults, teenagers or adult children do not want anything to do with them. In fact, there are parents who as a matter of fact also hate their children, or are ashamed of them and do not want anything to do with them. In essence, they have 'divorced' them; the relationship is estranged. You might be one of them or you may consider yourself as getting there or you may think that this does not apply to you or you might know someone in that position. Please continue to read on and journey with me and I pray that you will be enlightened and empowered to inform your own situation.

I ask the question, why the divorce? Why the estranged relationship? Why should it come to that? I mean, you and I carried our babies for up to 9 months sometimes over, then we had to go through the excruciating pain of labour to birth them, then parent them as our princesses and princes only for them to grow up and not want anything to do with us? How come? Sadly, my daughter and her father have 'divorced' each other. I would have been 'divorced' too, had I not retraced my steps to the truth and the principles thereof. I had to make the choice to change and grow with the knowledge and experience.

So, if 'the fruit of the womb is a reward' like scripture says, what I was seeing from my daughter prior to my taking my parenting apprenticeship seriously was certainly not a reward. I did not know what it was, but it was certainly was not a reward. I had leaned on my own understanding and the result was a disaster. I had to unlearn that and relearn the way of the truth.

My Source: The Truth

Whatever you believe to be the source of your existence, you need the help of a supernatural force. Be it God, Allah, Buddha or whoever or whatever you believe to control your existence or who gives you life: you will definitely need their help. Believe me, doing it on your own strength would take you so far because your ability and strength is limited without your source. Again, your own understanding and efforts is limited of the bigger picture. It will get to a point that the fire inside you may dwindle or go out at some point because of its limitation and you would need that super power to rekindle your fire and keep it aglow. I know of only one Super Power who is God. I am blessed to experience Him and to be able to share with you. He is my source and this is my TRUTH.

As I have already established, I had done parenting in my own way and strength. I did not know the Truth. How do I know how to parent if I didn't ask and learn from the Author or the Source, that is the One who created and instituted parenthood and employed me as an apprentice to show me the way to do it successfully? I would act in ignorance, follow what everyone else is doing, thinking that is the way. I am highlighting again that when you have enough people behaving in a specific manner or way, that behaviour or mannerism soon become recognise as 'normal'. But the question is, is that the truth or the right way? The truth did not change because I chose to behave in a different way. The truth did not change because I was ignorant. The truth will not change for me or anyone else.

When you buy a piece of equipment or a gadget, you read the manual to learn how to operate it. At first you are a novice; my son would say "a noob"; you gradually learn how to use and operate the machine and you refer to the manual from time to time when needed. Similarly, I have come to the realisation that as parents, we need to learn how to nurture from the Creator's manual. When I decided to turn things around and became intentional with the parenting apprenticeship career, I was directed to look at the bigger picture by having the Creator at the centre. God is Omnipresent that means He is everywhere, He is Omniscient, meaning He is all-knowing and sees the bigger picture. He also knows the end from the beginning. He sees where my sight cannot reach and knows where I lack understanding. It is a no brainer to learn and depend on Him. I decided to learn from Him, as an apprentice would from his or her supervisor or manager who also employs him or her. This is my secret: I have learned that in life, I cannot live a meaningful and fulfilling life outside of my Creator who is my Source. From this perspective I have been blessed to view all my errors in judgement, wrong choices, mistakes as learning experiences or opportunities for growth not failures.

If you have not already figured out who I am learning from, then here we go. I am delighted to share with you that I am learning from God who is my also my Father, by the power of His Holy Spirit through His son Jesus Christ of Nazareth. You must be wondering by now, how to become a committed apprentice? Well, let me put your mind at rest. You do not require to complete an application form or upload your CV or have an interview to be accepted into the apprenticeship course. You are already enrolled into the apprenticeship just by being a parent. To become committed you have to go through a few steps that I recommend:

1. *Respond to the call*

I had a call within my spirit when I hit rock bottom in my situation and I responded. You do not have to wait till you hit rock bottom before you respond. As you share my story right now, it could you be your call to discover the blessing of becoming a committed apprentice of parenthood. It is up to you whether you respond or not. This could be your only chance of making changes to find peace in your life. Will you give yourself the opportunity? "I stand at the door and knock, if anyone hears my voice and opens, then I will come in..." – Revelations 3:20. Jesus does not force you to accept Him and His ways. I can assure you that when you do, you are on your way to freedom and peace!

2. *Recognise and accept that God gave you your children.*

Your children are a heritage from the Lord (Psalm 127:3). They are good gifts and perfect gifts from the Lord (James 1:17). You can only cultivate and nurture the goodness in your children by being in tune with your Source and the Source of your children – God.

3. *Be in the presence of God*

Build and maintain a personal relationship with God through Jesus. Get to know God for yourself. Be hungry for Him. Build a relationship through prayer and meditation with the Jesus through the Holy Spirit. It is just like relating to a friend. The more you spend together chatting and talking, and sharing your life, the more you get closer. Jesus is your friend; you can talk with Him anywhere anytime. The presence of God is everything.

4. *Be prepared to discover God's plans by yourself*

As a parenting apprentice, commit to discovering God's plans for you and your children yourself not through anyone or second-hand information. You may be guided as to how to do it such as I am sharing with you right now. You may read good books and listen to good mentors. But you must go get it yourself. You experience God in your apprenticeship journey by yourself. My experience will be different from yours because He created me unique, and His plans for me are unique and so my journey is unique. So, is yours. You taste the Lord for yourself (Psalm 34:8) and come to your own conclusions; is He good? Is He sweet? Is He sour? Is He sweet and sour? You be the judge of that. And you can hold onto the promise in Jeremiah 29:13 that you will find the Lord when you seek and search Him with all your heart.

5. *Recognise God's voice*

As you engage in your relationship and friendship with Jesus, it is important that you are able to hear and recognise His voice. A conversation is a two-way thing. It is not enough to do all the talking without receiving from your friend. Recognising God's voice is not an automatic thing once you decide to become a committed apprentice. It is something that you develop and grow over time. God is patient; He will work with you to grow it. God can speak to you in so many ways. Sometimes in a thunderous voice as the case was with Moses from the Bible; other times in a still small voice. Sometimes in the whistles of the wind; other times just by the observation of things around you – nature. You cannot place a limit on God or underestimate Him. He can speak to you through your Bible; through those qualified to teach His Word; through a song; through your dreams; through a painful situation; through your thoughts and desires when you are submitted to Him. He can speak to you through your name. He communicates with me through my name all the time. My name means victory and anytime I require a boost of confidence, I am reminded that God said He has given me victory through His Son, Jesus and that was why He named me Eunice. The key to hearing God's voice is to stay close and keep your dial tuned to the Holy Spirit. It's like Wi-Fi. You have to be connected to the wi-Fi to receive. Just as you have to tune to the radio station to be able to hear what is being broadcasted, so you also tune to the Holy Spirit to hear what he is saying to you.

6. *Obedience*

Being a committed apprentice requires you to trust and obey and respond timely because procrastination and doubts work against you. The enemy uses these to delay you in your progression to rewards and blessings such as peace, joy and hope. I always reflect on the story of Elijah, who was a prophet of God in the Bible. You could read the story in 1 Kings 17 for yourself. Allow me to give you a gist of it. It happened one day; Elijah declared that there would be no rain in the land of Israel. God then directed Elijah to go to Brook Cherith and stay there by the brook because He has commanded the ravens to feed him there. Elijah could drink from the brook and the ravens will feed him. Elijah listened and obeyed the instructions of the Lord. Now, if Elijah had done what he thought was best for him based on his own wisdom and understanding, he would have missed the miracle of his life. If he had said, "I would go next week or I would go where I wanted to", he would have missed out on the provision. In Proverbs 3:5-6 says that *"Trust in the Lord your God with all your heart and lean not on your own understanding, in all your ways acknowledge him and he shall guide your paths."*

So it was that Elijah stayed at the Brook Cherith until the brook dried up. As soon as the brook dried up, God said to him go to the town called Zarephath for I have arranged for a widow and her son to feed you. Before the brook dried up, God had already planned for Elijah. God has called you into parenthood. He will always provide; He will always come through but you have to trust and obey. Will you trust and obey? As I walk you through my journey as a committed apprentice, you will share in other examples from my story. I trust God to do as He has promised and you can too. His promise is that His plans are not of evil, neither are they to destroy you; but to give you hope and a future (Jeremiah 29:11). As a committed apprentice who has gone through these steps that I share with you, I have come to the conclusion that God is good...all the time! *"The ways of the Lord are right; the righteous walk in them, but the transgressors stumble in them"* – *Hosea 14:9.*

Now that I have explored with you how to become a committed apprentice, I think it is time to introduce you to modules and lessons in the coming chapters. Let me prompt you though, the modules and lessons as outlined are not necessarily in order that I learned them. I have just put them in this order for easy organisation. I will end this chapter by sharing that I chose to learn from the best because He sees the bigger picture and He has the plan.

'For as the heavens are higher than the earth, so are My ways higher than your ways, and My thoughts than your thoughts.' – *Isaiah 55:9*

Modules

Here I am. I find myself in the classroom again, except that this classroom is not a building. Learning is taking place simultaneously within me; within my spirit, soul and body. I learned to harmonise 13 lessons across 3 modules simultaneously.

Module 1:

BUILDING A SOLID FOUNDATION

Solid foundation can withstand anything. Troubles and tribulations, test and trials will come. But you will stand with a solid foundation. If the foundation is weak, no matter how beautiful or expensive the building is, it will ultimately c ome tumbling down because the groundings are weak. The same thing applies to the nurturing of our children, no matter how good your intentions when the foundation is weak your efforts will ultimately not achieve what you want to. That was the situation I found myself.

> *'Be a wise man who built his house on the rock, and the rain descended, the floods came, and the winds blew and beat on that house, and it did not fall for it was founded on the rock.'*
> *– Matthew 7:24-25*

Chapter 4

Lesson 1: Spirit Soul Body

Now, let make things clear: I am a parenting apprentice and I have resolved to be a committed and good student. I quickly became familiarised with the scripture that says,

'Seek first the kingdom of God and His righteousness and all other things shall be added.' – Matthew 6:33

I established for myself that the Holy Spirit is my Supervisor, Jesus Christ of Nazareth is my Manager and God is the CEO. One of the first things I was taught was the truth about the spirit, soul and body. I already had the knowledge that indeed, as human beings we are made up of three beings; spirit, soul and body. I knew that much. What I did not fully comprehend was that these 3 beings are so important that we as human beings have to learn to operate and harmonise all 3 for an effective life. More often than not, we operate from the physical and forget about the spirit and soul of our being and situation. Of course, generally I hear people talk about, meeting or wanting to meet their soulmates. Even in this context, many people define this based on a physical premise. This is because the physical is so overwhelming and we consider the physical to be more compelling. We say, "Seeing is believing." When we live from just the physical, we run into lots of trouble, unaware and unprepared and we feel lonely, afraid and overwhelmed. I am not implying that we will not meet trouble or be tested on our life journey when we operate from the spirit, soul and body, but the difference is that although we are tested and trouble may come, we are never alone; and we may even be warned through dreams and revelations and prepared before some of the troubles come.

As I began to be an attentive and a committed apprentice, my Supervisor taught me to understand that knowing the order of priority was also important. I was educated that, things that manifest in the physical, first takes place in the spiritual. This is serious because operating only from the physical is not only ignorant, it is dangerous too. For me, the more I journey and learn from my Supervisor, the Holy Spirit, the more my relationship with God through prayer, communication and interactions and reading His Word are very crucial. I was led to comprehend that my relationship with God, being in His presence and being in tune with Him is paramount. In a nutshell, that is the first priority. Hence, 'Seek first the Kingdom of God and His righteousness...' God is Spirit and He relates to us through our spirit beings. That is why He created us in His image so that we will be of the same essence and enable the relationship between us and Him. So, it would be rather unfruitful for God to teach me when I am only operating from the physical. I cannot learn from Him without being in tune spiritually. Prior to my commitment to the apprenticeship, I had been operating only from the physical. I hope I am making sense. I can say with confidence that I have encountered many parents who are also operating from the physical. And the results are not favourable either.

If you recollect from earlier, I shared with you about the fact that I was feeling the full weight of what was happening in my situation, when I depended on my own strength. It was because I was operating from the physical. When we operate only from the physical, we have no support, no back-up, and no foundation. Therefore, we would feel the whole strain. However, when I drew closer to God, that took care of the spirit and the soul also fell into place, so that I operated from all three beings of my life.

Talking about soul falling into place, many people find it difficult to understand what the soul is. I would like to explain: when we dream in our sleep, it is our souls that is doing and seeing the things we do and see in our dreams. Our dreams take place in the spiritual realm. As an apprentice, I see the fact that I was and I am blessed with meaningful dreams that manifested in the physical as miracles. Yes! They are miracles. I could actually remember my dreams when I woke up in the mornings and that gave me the opportunity to have my dreams interpreted for my understanding so that I would be diligent and not act in ignorance. This was very helpful because it gave me direction to some situations. The troubles were still present and the level of difficulty was also present, but I did not feel the full strain of what was happening in my life and situation. I felt the amazing presence of God with me through the Holy Spirit who was and is constant with me through my reflections. Things became clearer to me, to the extent that sometimes I saw what was going to happen in a dream before it happened so I was in a way prepared. Is this not amazing? It is astounding because this is what God says in Psalm 32:8, "I will instruct you and teach you in the way you should go; I will guide you with My eye". It was intense. Consequently, whatever it was, when it eventually happened, of course, my physical body felt some impact. However, knowing that I was not alone, knowing that Jesus was and is with me, gave me the spiritual hope which ensured that my soul was at peace and enabled my physical strength to endure in the face of trouble. The spirit, soul and body working harmoniously. Sometimes I was forewarned through my dreams and given the opportunity to make a decision for when the occurrence actually happened. It was as though I knew what was going to happen so I was not utterly surprised when it actually did. That in a way also kept me grounded. Bringing the spiritual into the physical. This is divine grace and it is fulfilling; and I enjoy this being a committed apprentice. It is amazing to be let in on what is on God's mind before it manifests:

'New things I declare; before it springs forth, I tell you of them.' – Psalm 42:9

Let me ask a question: When was the last time you had a dream, remembered the dream and took it seriously? I am not talking about day dreaming. I am talking about going to bed and waking up from sleep with the story of where your soul has been whilst you were sleeping. I am talking about waking up with a dream like Joseph did and like the Pharoah of Egypt did. That kind of dream is what I am talking about. I am not saying that God communicates with us only through dreams, there are various ways. However, I think dreams are pretty effective because everyone sleeps – unless you suffer from insomnia. I will encourage you to be a committed apprentice and put your spirit, soul and body in order.

As I continued to learn, develop and grow in understanding, I made the declaration that: *'As for me and my household, we shall serve the Lord.' – Joshua 24:15.*

I have come to the conclusion that I cannot live my life apart from God and have any meaningful or fulfilling life. In fact, as human beings we cannot function effectively living apart from our Creator. We obtain our nourishment from the Creator as Jesus illustrated in John 15. He is the vine and we are the branches. The branches have to stay put on the vine in order to have the nutrition to grow, flourish and yield fruits. If I have been enlightened with the truth that I cannot live apart from God then I have to teach my children the same. I have to enlighten my children with the same truth so that they may also have purposeful and fulfilling lives. And if they were able to understand and accept this for their lives then they would do same for their own children. For me this is a legacy which is far more important than any material heritage. I would rather get this one right rather than leave them huge sums of money in the bank as inheritance.

I knew that I couldn't achieve this on my own. I needed direction and help from my supervisor. The earlier you as a parent bring your children to God the better. In essence the earlier you start to take the apprenticeship seriously the better. However, here I was having to start with 2 maturing adults or teenagers. I had to start this from scratch. Prior to this, I did occasionally go to catholic mass with my children when they were younger but I took them for the wrong reason. Let me confess: the reason being to get them into catholic schools. Yes, I said it! It is shameful but that is the truth. I am very sorry; many parents were doing it so I did it too. How awful. So, I was not diligent and certainly not intentional about what I was doing in terms of their salvation or Jesus dying for their sins. Now as a committed apprentice, I have a new perspective. I had to start doing this intentionally and in the right manner and truthfully. I had to be committed if I wanted my children to be committed.

My son, was around 9 years at the time, so he was still compliant to some extent. He was a lot more flexible. He came to Sunday mass with me regularly. However, my daughter, was much older, about 15 nearly 16 years old, she was hesitant and reluctant at that time. She did however come with her brother and I on a few occasions with her face telling the story of, "I do not want to be here." I remember we would go for brunch after mass which my daughter and son both enjoyed. That was my way of getting them to come to mass. You may call it bribery. It was my way of giving us something to look forward to after mass. It was such a chore getting my daughter to come to mass. Eventually I decided to stop 'making' her come with us. I came to the realisation that at the right time she would come back. I was empowered as I was directed to draw on the promise of God that says:

> *'Refrain your voice from weeping and your eyes from tears: for your work shall be rewarded, says the Lord. And they shall come back from the land of the enemy. There is hope in your future, says the Lord, that your children shall come back to their own border.' – Jeremiah 31:16-17.*

I continue to pray for my children's salvation. Sometimes you have to know when to back off physically and battle in the spirit through prayer. This is another truth I have learnt as an apprentice. The Holy Spirit directed me to be prepared for when my daughter and son begin to ask spiritual questions. I knew that I could not give what I didn't have and I couldn't teach what I didn't know. To be able to do this effectively, I had to learn for myself and then I would be able to teach them. This meant to spend time in the Word of God and build my relationship with God.

We gain wisdom from God when we draw closer to Him. In November, 2020, my daughter shared with her brother and I that she felt that she was immortal. My son and I listened to her as she talked. The first thing that came to my mind was, that was impossible, God alone is immortal. I did not say that to her of course! I continued to listen and commented, "That was interesting", at the end. My son on the other hand had discernment, understanding and explained, "She thinks and feels like she is immortal because of the things she has been through and done to herself, and through all that she is still here and alive." I thought wow that was wisdom, I didn't think about that, and reading from my daughter's face I could tell that she was in agreement with her brother. Now, let me highlight here that, many a time, many adults think that they are the only ones with wisdom and understanding and not children because of their experience. Yes, adults may have experience due to their age compared to children and young people. However, wisdom and understanding come from God and He gives these to anyone that He wants, including children and teenagers too. As parents we must learn to recognise this.

My daughter went on to say that this feeling of being immortal makes her think about and ask about what is her purpose on this earth plane. I listened to her and her brother without interrupting them and then when I heard her say 'purpose', I saw a direction. It was like an ignition inside me. I felt within my spirit that there was more to this than just talk. I came out to comment that I did not think about purpose in the same sense that she was thinking about, when I was her age. Of course, I used the word but not with the context and meaning that she was using it. I shared this with her and her brother. God gave me the wisdom and understanding to comprehend the connection between feeling immortal and her purpose. Now that brought joy and peace to my soul. I praised my CEO; I praised my Manager and I praised my Supervisor. Then I had to wait for the right time to explain what I felt within my spirit with regards to her being immortal and her purpose. As an apprentice, I have to be spiritually in tune with the Holy Spirit, to receive enlightenment, understanding and wisdom. Then I have to wait for the physical timing to be right before acting. This is the spirit, soul and body working together. I have learned to harmonise the spirit, soul and body through my apprenticeship.

I am grateful and humbled that I can share my apprenticeship journey with you in this manner. Being a committed apprentice has made a real difference because not only do I enjoy being in the presence of God, God has blessed me with wisdom and I have also been able to love my teenagers unconditionally. I see the hand of God behind the things that happen in my life. I will encourage you to decide today to take your parenting apprenticeship seriously; to unlearn, re-learn, apply and grow to '...bear much fruit' (John 15:5). Be a committed apprentice. I will close this chapter with this verse I love so much. I cannot do it on my own and guess what, the truth is you cannot do it on your own either:

> *'Unless the Lord builds the house, they labour in vain who builds it. Unless the Lord guards the city, the watchman stays awake in vain.' – Psalm 127:1*

Chapter 5

Lesson 2: Parenting v Nurturing

Being an apprentice, has enabled me to be intentional and purposeful in the way I live and nurture my maturing adults. My Supervisor has nurtured my senses over time through the renewal of my mind. It is brilliantly amazing. My sight and vision, hearing, my spiritual intuition (feel) and understanding (mindset) have been enhanced. Consequently, I can say that I apply wisdom in the way I live and nurture my teenagers. I have been challenged and encouraged to question a lot of things. There are some words and phrases that I have questioned their real meaning and their application and place in my life and my relationship with others. Words such as 'compromise', 'no one is perfect', 'submission' among others. And each time I have been led and guided on a thorough journey of reflections to arrive at a different perspective.

Today I am questioning 'parenting'. I am questioning parenting because for me, the word is limited in a lot of ways. No wonder many parents are doing the same things and doing a bad job at it. Society is doing a bad job at it, looking at the results. I did a bad job at it when I was parenting like the world taught me. Many parents are parenting just as I did because we all do not know any better. As I mentioned before, late 2016, I began to question the way I was doing things in my life because the results were not desirable. I am blessed to be able to say that I have undergone and continue to go through learning and development which is resulting in my growth as an apprentice. I am growing and I know I have grown from where I come from. My Supervisor gives me feedback and confirms it through my teenagers. Isn't that amazing! I don't worry about what people are thinking because I am being trained by the best. I am covered!

I have been taught and learned to nurture rather than parent. I went through a few teething problems. It was a new skill and I had to give myself time to learn and apply, just as I would if I was learning a new course or a module. As I have been patient and consistent, I have made progress which is yielding fruits. I gained the understanding that parenting not only put the emphasis on the parent, for me, it also assumes that the parenting style that one adopts should fit all. One style fits all! As we know, even in a family, the same parenting style does not benefit all the children in the family, not even identical twins. The simple reason being, every child is different. I knew this alright and I am sure many parents do too. Nonetheless, for some reason our default is to parent our children in the same way. That is why sometimes we hear of parents who may say, "What did we do different with this child?" when the child in question does not turn out like the other 'good' child. The answer to that question is simply, "What didn't you do differently? It is because we parent our children in the same manner. We seldom do anything different. For example, consider the family of doctors. Grandparents are doctors, parents are doctors, now the 2 grandchildren must most definitely be parented to become doctors too. One grandchild may well thrive as a doctor however, the other may struggle to become the doctor but might be miserable for the rest of his or her life. This is blanket parenting. Or if he or she failed to become a doctor, then he or she becomes the 'failure' in the family; the bad nut in the family; the disgrace in the family.

I believe that because we are so busy parenting, it is easy for us to employ the parenting style or skills of our parents to parent our own children especially from where I come from. Again, blanket parenting. It is even more heart-breaking to see that we are so convinced that those styles must work because they worked on us. Even when it is so clear they are not working; we still insist on the same parenting skills. I believe that some people actually think that because they provide food, shelter, clothes and education, they are parenting and that is enough for their children. Look around you and see the results of parenting; in your own home, in the community and in society. What picture do you see? What painting do you see? I tell you what I see: I see 'leave-it-to-chance' parenting; I see parents rushed off their feet, I see parents too busy and I see teenagers feeling 'neglected' and feeling unloved. I see chaos; I see pandemonium. I see unfruitfulness. I see it vividly because I have been there.

Let me challenge you today to nurture instead of parent. First, I was enlightened and I was challenged to do it. Then, I accepted the challenge and I finally ran with it. I must point out that I am where I am because I accepted the responsibility to be a committed apprentice. Today, I am challenging you, what is it going to be? Parenting or nurturing? Before you decide, let me enlighten you.

Nurturing for me, has a broader, more meaningful and challenging aspects that can actually enable child rearing to be fulfilling and rewarding. Think about it, when we say parenting, what comes to your mind? Take a minute to think about it. For me, nothing visual apart from the word 'parent' or an 'adult' or 'authority.' Now look at nurturing. As soon as I hear the word, I see grow or growth; I see a plant or a flower; I think of taking care of something to maturity; I see love. Nurturing compels me to look at the totality of the child. For me it put the emphasis on the child rather than me (the parent). When I think about nurturing my child, I think about cultivation.

Take a look at cultivating maize for instance. We take into account a lot of factors in order to make sure the maize mature for a good harvest. We for instance look at the soil, weather conditions, the right season or time to cultivate, the manure or fertilizer, water, pest and weed control and who will be responsible for the day-to-day tendering and caring for the maize. We even take into account the needs of the maize at every developmental stage of its growth. There may even be contingency plans (how to water the maize in the absence of rain for example) to ensure the maturation, fruits and good harvest. We consider all these factors even before we put the first maize seed into the soil. Mind you, when we want to cultivate potatoes as a second crop, we may arrive at different results for the same considerations above. Why? Because they are two different crops that have different needs. And even the farmer has to have some training for the cultivation by learning from someone who knows how to. Or even if we buy flower seeds from the supermarket, we have to follow the instructions on the packaging. So, my previous question comes in again, "Who are you learning from or who are you taking instructions from?"

When it comes to having babies, most people do not plan a baby let alone to take into account all the factors to cultivate (nurture) a child. Of course, we may sort out the crib, the clothes, the pram, food, nappies and the like to welcome the baby into the world. These are just scratching the surface. I admit I was one of these parents. I got pregnant even before I could think about the implications of having a baby. Of course, I did not plan my baby, however it is so true that my CEO did. I mean God did and He had a plan for my children even before they were born. God has plans for your children and young people too. You only have to ask Him and He will reveal them to you. It is important however that you become a committed apprentice, otherwise you will not be able to hear Him when He tells you. When I had my baby, my daughter, I was determined to do my best. I worked hard to put food on the table. I worked hard to put clothes on her back. I worked hard to drop her to breakfast club and to collect her after school. I worked hard to pay the baby sitter and au-pair fees. I worked hard to buy her the toys to play with. I worked hard to put her through extra tuition. I worked hard to provide her with the birthday parties. You name it. This was what I called parenting. I did do my best at parenting as I would imagine many parents do, only to realised later that I was just scratching the tip of the iceberg. I realised that the parenting, which I now call 'everyday parenting or leave-it-chance parenting' is nothing compared to what it is supposed to be. What I was supposed to be doing was nurturing.

I found the truth because I became a diligent student who studied as I would for a new course. I was directed to research and asked questions, reflections and reading. I read a lot and my Supervisor encouraged me. It is so sad and unfortunate that we as parents are so busy that we do not have the time for nurturing. Our children need our time. Through all the training, I realised that 'nurturing' is what I was supposed to be doing as a mother. But of course, I thought that I was nurturing my children when I was parenting them. I began to discover more and more through research and finally I came to the conclusion that nurturing is what I have not been doing. I decided to unlearn parenting to relearn nurturing as a mother for my children.

My children were older by now so it was tough nurturing them but I was determined to do that. I struggled a lot with 'too late syndrome' especially from my daughter who was now well into her teen years. 'Too late syndrome' in simple terms means that I had left things too late and so I had to be prepared for some intense and disheartening challenges. Yes! I mean intense. Intense in every sense of the word. I struggled because I had to go through the heartache of undoing the results of the wrong 'parenting' that I had done since my children's birth before I could lay new foundations; prepare the soil to receive new seeds for cultivation (nurturing). It was tough, difficult and complex but worthwhile and I would encourage anyone to go through nurturing. My secret though was drawing strength from Jesus Christ (my Manager) through the Holy Spirit (my Supervisor). I could do it because I found my identity in my Creator. I could do it because I became a diligent and committed apprentice.

Nurturing, as I have already stated for me, focuses on the child. So, for me, nurturing my teenagers, means that I have two separate individuals to focus on. That is, two different seeds to nurture and grow. I had to take into account the environmental factors, their ages and their developmental stages into account, their personalities and most importantly for me how they receive love as individuals. For me, I had to learn how to:

1) build a nurturing environment.

2) My daughter is six and half years older than her brother, so that meant two different sets of nurturing needs to take into account. She was in her teenage years whilst my son was approaching his adolescence. My daughter at this time, I believe was an angry teenager; she was hurt and felt unloved. She was in what I call the 'I don't care mode'. You were lucky if you got any word out of her. It was either monosyllables or 'I don't care'. I didn't know her; she was like an 'alien.' Looking at her behaviour at home, it was simple to make the easy choice to conclude that she was rude, disrespectful or disobedient. However, one would require insight and grace to fully understand

who this 'alien' was, and where this 'alien' had come from. My son on the other hand was young so was relatively compliant, however he was very observant and can be tearful at times. I certainly did not want another alien in my son too. So, again two different nurturing needs to take into account.

3) I had to learn how my daughter interpreted and received love and I had to do the same for my son. I learnt that my daughter and son interpreted and received love differently. In effect, I had to determine what their primary love languages are, and to learn and intentionally speak their primary love languages and communicate it to them.

Creating a nurturing environment: soil

My task was to create a soil for nurturing my two crops so to speak. To create a nurturing environment, that is an environment that supports cultivation and growth for my daughter and my son, I have to be a nurturing parent. So, then who is a nurturing parent? What goes into becoming a nurturing parent? I was directed to the work of Dr Gary Chapman. In his book, *The 5 Love Languages of Teenagers: The Secrets to Loving Teens Effectively,* I learned that a nurturing parent is a parent who creates a supportive and positive environment and atmosphere for teenagers and children to thrive. I understood again that a nurturing parent has a positive attitude and entertain positive thoughts and looks for ways to improve the lives of their children. When I discovered these truths about a nurturing parent, I realised that the environment my daughter, son and I were in at the time was far from nurturing. The environment was inconsistent: sometimes OK but other times argumentative, shouting, stressful and unhappiness. Our attitude as parents (my children's father and I were married and living together at the time) was negative and our language was negative too. In a nut shell, because we were not nurturing parents, we could not create a nurturing environment. And why were we not nurturing parents? It was because we had taken matters into our own hands, parenting 'anyhow'. We were doing a job that required us to be under supervision but we were operating without a supervisor. We were ignorant of that truth.

Immediately, I realised that even before I could begin to nurture my children in the way and manner that they ought to be I had to look at myself. I had to evaluate myself, review my attitude, my behaviours, thoughts, to have a positive mindset. That was when I was directed to this:

'Do not conform to this world, but be transformed by the renewing of your mind that you may prove what is that good, and acceptable and perfect will of God.' – Romans 12:2

I have to review where I had come from, where I am and where I wanted to be in raising my children. I concluded that I could only achieve that through nurturing. I could only be successful through my apprenticeship. Immediately I realised that I had to turn the volume of my voice down and also to change from negative words to positive words. I shouted because I was frustrated. I was frustrated because my daughter was not doing what I expected her to do. I was frustrated because the more I 'corrected' her the more she made 'mistakes'. The more she made mistakes the more I used negative words and critical words. I was using negative words because I had trained my mind to only see the things that she did wrong. I was afraid that if I did not correct her then she might not make it in the outside world. I had to change that negative perspective to a positive one. That comes through renewing of mind, and it was only the Holy Spirit that helped me to achieve that.

The environment is made up of the home environment and the wider environment of the community and society at large. The environment I was able to control as a parent when it comes to nurturing was the home environment. I appreciated that it was from the home environment that my daughter and my son would develop the skills to thrive in the wider environment. However, I had to take the implications of the wider environment into account when creating a nurturing environment.

So, immediately I knew that parenting like my parents will not get me where I wanted to get to because I was raised in a totally different environment, where the same parenting style was adopted for all the children in the family. Now, the fact that the parenting style 'appeared' to have worked with all my siblings, could not be the basis for me to use the same parenting style for my own children, although that is what many parents tend to do. We may think that it had worked, however if we would reflect on ourselves and lives, we might arrive at different conclusions. We might recognise that there were deficiencies in our lives that could be attributed to the one-size-fit-all parenting we received. We default into adopting our parents parenting strategies regardless. What I have seen happen was that we refuse to change the style even though we could see that it was not working. We become frustrated, exhausted and stressed in the process. In the end we produce emotionally depleted young people who not only hate us as parents but hate their own lives as they struggle to survive in the wider community. I have learned that an emotionally stable child with a supportive foundation (roots) can soar in the wider world. I wanted that for my daughter and my son.

Creating a nurturing home environment for me was a difficult task; a very challenging task. Why? I started the apprenticeship career on my own as my now ex-husband was not ready to change from the 'old style parenting'. To make matters worse we were experiencing marital difficulties which impacted the relationship between us parents and also with my daughter. Believe me it was difficult doing it on my own, not because I was a single parent, but because whenever I made progress with my daughter, my husband's 'old parenting strategies' sabotaged the progress. That created inconsistencies in the home environment.

Needs for nurturing: Love

With a supportive and positive environment, the needs of individual child are to be explored and nurtured for optimal growth. Now remember, as mentioned the needs might be different for every child in your household because according to Gary Chapman human beings receive love in 5 different ways, he calls these languages. According to him each individual has a love language that when spoken with him or her, he or she interprets as love and consequently fills their emotional love tank. The lack of an individual receiving love in this manner means that their emotional love tank is depleted to the extent that they feel unloved regardless of whatever you do for them; consequently, affecting their whole life adversely.

The love languages are, words of affirmation, gifts, acts of service, quality time and personal touch. A nurturing parent must learn to speak the primary language of each and every child and teenager in the family effectively for them to receive and feel loved. However, children and teenagers require sprinkling of the rest of the love languages in order to thrive and build a strong emotional love that will enable them to thrive in the wider world.

I found this book by Gary Chapman very useful. I quickly learned the love languages of my daughter and my son. It was easy to determine the love language for my son. He is a touchy-feeler person. His primary love language is physical touch. If you asked him, "How do you know that mummy loves you?" he would say, "she cuddles me and gives me lots of hugs." He also enjoys his soft teddy bears and blanket. It was fairly easy to ascertain his love language. My daughter on the other hand, was the challenge. I went through a questionnaire with her to assess her love language and came out with gifts (she was at a stage that she could be manipulative and she was beginning to like money), however I felt that 'words of affirmation' and 'acts of service' have worked tremendously with her. I will talk more about love languages in a different chapter later in this book. Although I was armed with their primary languages, I soon realised that doing the task ahead on my own strength was not only difficult but impossible. That is why it is useful to be a committed apprentice. Because as an apprentice whenever you encounter any difficult or challenging tasks, you have the support of your supervisor. So that was it and is still is for me. I took my difficulties and challenges to Him for discussion and directions. Sometimes He might say, "Go ahead and implement A B C or D." Other times He might say, "I will take care of it." *'Be still and know that I am God' (Psalm 46:10).* How refreshing! My identity is in God. I know that God gave me my daughter and my son, I comprehended that He is the One to help and teach me the way. He alone knows how and could teach me to nurture them the way they ought to be. I understood that He is leading me to nurturing my teenagers successfully and, in a fulfilling, and rewarding manner. Allowing God and for that matter the Holy Spirit through Jesus Christ into my situation, changed things. Don't get me wrong, the difficulty was there because of starting late in the apprenticeship commitment, and the problems were present but I found the strength to carry on and move forward. Remember I described 'too late syndrome' to you earlier. Through my apprenticeship, I was enlightened to understand that God's grace is readily available to all of us, however we have to tune in like we tune into a radio station, to experience it and enjoy the full benefits thereof. As I intentionally tuned in to tap into the grace, I was strengthened with the patience, the endurance, the long suffering, the consistency, the perseverance, hope and the peace to journey on to nurturing my maturing adults.

For my journey, I was determined to learn to be a nurturing mother. I am blessed to be a fast learner and whenever I was directed to something that would develop and grow me, I embarked on it. I didn't waste time. I still do that now. The only time I would wait was when my Supervisor, directed me to do so. Or sometimes I was directed to know that something must be dealt with spiritually and not physically. So, within no time I was intentional about nurturing my teenagers and I was learning every day and putting into practice what I learn. I was attentive and intentional but boy, it was difficult sometimes because I had 15 years of catch-up learning and practice to do, but I persevered. I got it wrong sometimes but I acknowledged it and got on with it. Somehow, I had hoped that the home environment would change but it remained volatile and consistently inconsistent. So, it made it even tougher. Now looking back; looking at where I am now with nurturing my daughter and my son, I can say that I would not have been able to progress this far living in the old environmental conditions. I can confidently say that by grace, I am blessed and favoured to enjoy peace and harmony in my home environment now (nurturing environment); my daughter is thriving and so is my son. My teenagers are doing so much better than when I was parenting. We have a better meaningful relationship and enjoy each other's company. I continue to nurture them and I'm also beginning to intentionally guide them to nurturing their own lives.

For me, nurturing is cultivation; and when it comes to growing children, it is nurturing for me! I am learning from the best to bear much fruit. What will it be for you?

> *'He who abides in Me and I in him bears much fruits; for without me you can do nothing.' – John 15:5*

Module 2:

BE INTENTIONAL

I have to view nurturing (parenting) as a career that develops over time. It is an apprenticeship career. It is important that nurturing of our children is intentional. The Holy spirit directed and taught me to be intentional. Intentional nurturing of my teenagers means that I am conscious in my efforts pertaining to the assessment of their needs, and my strategies that I implement. Intentional in the sense that I don't leave nurturing to chance but plan, implement, review and evaluate my strategies. I am also intentional about the fact that I am harmonising the spirit, soul and body. I have learned how to do this through reflection and communication with my Supervisor by being a committed apprentice.

Chapter 6

Lesson 3: Unlearn to Relearn

Research points to the fact that the most important influence in the life of a child or teenager comes from his/her parents. So, then, I asked the question: when our relationship with my daughter was so estranged that she has shut down; would not communicate her feelings and thoughts with us; when she viewed us as her 'enemy of her progress'; did not trust our words or opinion and shuts us out of her life; what could we do? Each encounter between my daughter and us was a confrontation which ended in emotional distress, then how do we become this most significant influence in her life? In our world today, the involvement of parents in teenagers' lives has become so detrimental. It is more important now than it ever used to be.

Our children live and are expected to navigate their lives in a technological everchanging world that is changing by the minute if not micro-second. What I am driving at is the fact that our children live in a global world with mobile phones, internet, satellites, television, among other social media. Have you heard the saying, "if you don't parent your child, someone else would parent him/her for you?" One thing I dreaded was not being involved in my children's lives. I dreaded it because if I become uninvolved or insignificant in my children's lives my main role of guidance will be replaced by someone else or something else. Can you think of any such replacement? Oh, I can: the government, gang, peers, social media or Twitter. Well, I don't know about you but I was not having it, because to me it meant that I have failed my apprenticeship.

I adopted a principle that I hold dearly when it comes to intentional nurturing. I was enlightened with this principle during my early months at being a committed to apprenticeship. I decided to be a loving leader in my home. You may say, "But I love my children." Yes, I did love my children but now I have a different approach to loving my teenagers. I love them consciously and serve as a loving leader to them in my home. In other words, my actions have to agree with my words. If I say I love my children and my actions do not communicate love to them, then I have not achieved anything. Take this scenario; in your marriage relationship, when you hear your husband tell you day in and day out that he loves you and yet his actions are far from what you interpret as love, do you feel loved? I bet you will be screaming to yourself, "if you love me then show it!" It is the same thing for our children and our teenagers. So, I had to learn ways to love them that communicated my love to them. I will share with you some of the ways I communicate love to my teenagers and loved ones for them to receive it later in module 3 of this book.

When I say a leader 'I don't mean the kind that demands, pushes and orders people around. Not the kind that expects others to act in one way and he/she another. When I say a leader, I mean the kind that will model the action for others to follow. So, for example I did not want my teenagers to shout, so, I had to adjust my own speaking volume to demonstrate to them. The kind that would knock on her teenager's door before entering her room to show or lead her to doing the same when entering yours. This also demonstrated respect for my teenagers. God respects us so much and does not force us to do things or disrespect our privacy. That is why Jesus says, 'I stand at the door and knock' (Revelation 3:20). Jesus knocks the door out of respect for me and waits for me to ask Him in because He also respects my free will. If Jesus does this for me, then I could learn to do it with joy for my teenagers too. Again, if you don't expect your child to swear, then don't swear. I don't want my children to smoke so I don't smoke. It is as simple as that. I am not saying that they might not learn to swear or smoke from somewhere; what I am saying is that they are not going to learn that from me and not from my home especially when I am saying it is not good for them. Ultimately a time comes when they have to be accountable for their own actions. When I tell my children one thing and I do something contrary, they would think that if what I was asking them to do was so good and beneficial, why am I not doing it myself? Actions speak louder to our teenagers than our words. That is how God designed us. We watch and do what we see. Jesus said that He did what He saw His Father did. And when He commissioned His disciples, He asked them to go out there to do as they had seen Him do. The same way our children also do what they see us do. Watch out for inconsistencies. We get away with our words and actions when our children were younger but we won't get away with it now that they are teenagers.

I have come to understand that our children face an enormous pressure to achieve; get the 'right' grades; and the 'right' school that parents presume would equip them for a job in an ever-changing economy. The pressures of getting into grammar schools and 11+ preparations and tests, pressures of getting good grades for Russell Group universities can be very demanding. I am not implying that good schools, or good grades or Russell Group universities are not good or not achievable. What I am saying is for you to be aware of the pressures that are involved in and the impact of such pressures. Such pressures create fear and anxiety in our children. My husband and I were so busy pushing our daughter in directions that, we did not recognise what it was doing to her. We also paid little attention to her natural abilities, talents, and gifts that really mattered to her. I have come to the understanding that many parents steer their children in different directions when they think that their gifts and talents will not get them anywhere in the economy. The fear (I did not realise at the time that it was fear) crippled us so much so that we became harsh and critical because we wanted her to succeed. I have learned that success is subjective; it means different things to different people. I define success differently now. For me, success is knowing your purpose and pursuing it to the best of your ability. That is what I call, 'running a good race'. That is success! I am sure you know what you consider success to be. You may come to a different conclusion of what success means when you become intentional and start your own journey of being a committed apprentice.

I remember my daughter always had to do routine homework in the morning before school and work after school. That was the routine for a very long time, at least until she went to secondary school. She was very academically able child. I mean she is academically able child. As she grew up it became harder to get her to do her routine work. I knew that she was reluctant to do the work, but I did not realise that she resented doing the work. I recall that she made an angry comment one day when she was in year 3 or 4. She said to me, "All you cared about was work." She was still in primary school then. She did her Kumon Math and English tutor programme and excelled. At the time I did not think much of it. Then she did not make it to the grammar school because she did not get the mark required during the 11+ exams. This is the selection exams they take in year 6 for grammar schools. The pressure we as her parents put on her was just too enormous, all in the name of preparing her for the future. I felt the pressure too. So, no wonder she thought and felt like a failure although we reassured her that it did not matter.

It has become clear to me that the criticisms and pressure might have moulded her emotional well-being the way she is at present. What we did not realise at the time was the fact that our actions were gradually stripping our child of her confidence. She lost her confidence. The once confident child lost it all. She begun having panic attacks at school especially during examinations. We as parents picked on all the 'negative things, we were critical of everything and gave little or no credit to the positives. Now don't get me wrong, we wanted the best for her and I believe that most parents if not all, want the best for their children, however our approach and strategy was faulty. We simply did not know how to do it. Our language as parents was negative and the few times where we were actually positive did not mean anything to her. At first she put so much pressure on herself to live up to our 'expectations' until she entered into the 'I don't care mood'.

My words had no meaning to her; she listened to her peers and their views were more important. Let me clarify that teenagers tend to listen and value the opinions of their peers anyways. However, when I, as her mother couldn't get any word in or didn't have a clue about my daughter's world, then I was in deep trouble. It meant my daughter became vulnerable, an easy target for social preys, risked being a dropout of school, run-away from home, gangs etc. As a parent I didn't want to lose my children. I didn't want to lose that guidance role. I had to unlearn to relearn quickly as a parent. I am sure that by now you can picture 'the state of our relationship'. Sometimes you don't realise how you get there but by the time you realise, you are there. You just see the results manifest; however, those results would have been brewing from years before.

So, you can understand and appreciate when I say that I had to embark on this road of intentional nurturing with or without my husband who was reluctant to changes at the time. I had to relearn quickly and I made the decision to move away from expecting and demanding my teenagers to be appreciative or show appreciation for what I did for them. Don't get me wrong, I am not saying that they didn't have to show appreciation, of course they did! But what I am saying is, I was not going to demand it. After all, I had taught them the manners and courtesy. They know right from wrong as proportionate to their age. My aim and focus were and still are to be a responsible and intentional in my role and purpose as a parent. I am of the view that my teenagers do not owe me anything. Believe me, that is what many of our teenagers if not all think, they might not say it to you but they think it and show it in their actions too. They think this way because of the way we are parenting them. Some teenagers feel that we as parents demand gratitude from them for what we do for them as though they owe us. To them the gratitude is the payback for what we do for them. To be fair, I think that is the way it comes across even though that might not be our intention. I mean, we got so frustrated because we thought our daughter was ungrateful. I know my daughter felt that way because she told me. I decided consciously or unconsciously to bring them into this world so I am responsible for them, no matter what. When I fulfil this role effectively, my teenagers would show appreciation willingly. Maybe not immediately or in the near future but I knew it would happen in the long run. I adopted a different approach and a different perspective. I changed my attitude!

> *"If you don't like something, then change it. If you can't change it, then change your attitude." – Maya Angelou*

One day, I asked my daughter to do something for me and her answer was, "NO! you don't own me". I was shocked but then it gave me insight into her thinking. I was glad that she actually came out with it. I considered such occurrence as gold nuggets because it gave me insight and understanding into her behaviour. I had only been able to do this because I took my apprenticeship seriously. This happened about 2 years into becoming a committed apprentice. You see the effects of 'too late syndrome'. Now that was hurtful and difficult but you know what, I was also toughened by the Holy Spirit.

I also discovered that when I compared the parenting I received and the one I was giving my children; it was easy to fall into the trap of expecting my teenagers to be grateful to me. I had found myself in this trap of comparing and expectation leading to training my mind to demand respect and gratitude and even more so, especially when they were not forth coming as I expected. Generally, people become upset and angry when their expectations are not fulfilled. This in turn creates further tension in the household relationships. I accepted that my teenagers do not owe me anything. Further analysis of my situation enabled me to come to a new conclusion and a healthy mindset. A mindset to do my duty and responsibility efficiently and effectively without expecting anything in return; to appreciate the privilege to be a parent; and be grateful for the opportunity to be a guide for my children. From this perspective, I receive 'job satisfaction and fulfilment for a job well done. The appreciation and gratitude from the children are bonus and the icing on the cake. I don't even like icing, so for me I would say the carnation milk in my tea. So be patient for it. Do not demand for it.

'And do not be conformed to this world, but be transformed by the renewing of your mind, that you may prove what is that good and acceptable and perfect will of God.' – Romans 12:2

Chapter 7

Lesson 4: Application of Knowledge

Consider these:

1. Who spends more time with my child whilst I am out on my 9-5?
   - Extended family?
   - Nursery?
   - Nanny?
   - Live-in au-pairs?

2. Who is actually parenting my children in their formative years? Is it me:
   - Who collects my child from the nanny when he/she is already asleep?
   - Who collects my child from the nursery when I am so exhausted that I get home only with enough energy to feed my child and put her to bed, only to begin the same routine the next day?
   - Who gets home when my child is already asleep?

I am sure that you can consider these questions carefully.

Let me share mine with you. I started working part-time in retail and part-time taking the NVQ in Microsoft Office course. My daughter was around 8months to a year old. My mother was baby-sitting my daughter when I was in college in the morning and at work in the evening. By the time I got home my daughter was asleep. My daughter and I were living together with her father. We lived quite far from my mother so we set off around 5am to get to my mother's as my daughter's father gave us lift on his way to work. I was not driving at the time. I would leave my mum's at around 9am to attend college. When I finished college around 3pm, I would quickly go to see my daughter and then, I would set off to my part-time job for a 7pm start. My partner (who became my husband and now my ex-husband) would collect my daughter on his way home from work in the evening. I finished work at 11pm and got home around midnight. I would have a few hours of sleep, then the whole routine started again the next day. I knew my daughter was safe with my mother but the question, I ask myself now is: who was parenting my daughter? She is my daughter, I am the one on the parenting apprenticeship course, but I know now that my parenting was left to chance and not intentional. I am not saying that I did the wrong thing or the right thing. I did what I thought was best at the time. Most parents, if not all parents, and society, consider this as normal, am I right? What I am saying is that actions have consequences. Without knowledge you would behave in ignorance. You would just follow the crowd.

> Without knowledge ignorance is inevitable.

From the time she was 8 months until March, 2018, when she was nearly 17 years old, I had either been in full time education and or employment. I had my share of live-in au pairs by the time my son (who was born in 2007) was two and half years old and started nursery. The point I am trying to make is that when I had an 'imposter', a 'monster' or an 'alien' in my home, I now appreciate from reflection that it was partly because I had done 'leave-it-to-chance parenting' or 'everyday parenting.' I realised that I had excelled in my 9-5 career and I sucked at the parenting career. That was the bottom line. It was a hard pill to swallow but it was just that!

Gathering information and gaining insight into the situation, I made the decision and choice to be an intentional mother. I decided to embark on the parenting apprenticeship from a whole new perspective. Oh! Guess what, it is a lot harder but very achievable. The author I mentioned before, Dr Munroe, described my kind of situation as 'too late syndrome' in his book, *Kingdom Parenting*. It was a lot harder because all the thorns on the soils had to be removed, and the land ploughed before new seed could be planted. Then the seed requires watering, nurturing and the right soil conditions to germinate, grow and bear fruits. Now this takes time. I hope you understand this analogy. It would be a lot easier if intentional nurturing starts right at the commencement of the parenting apprenticeship. Even before the conception and arrival of the child. I mean nurturing is not easy but I believe it would be much more enjoyable if the beginnings and the foundations are right and firmly rooted.

Intentional nurturing for me, began with an apology to my children. First, I apologised to them individually and then together. I was specific about why I was apologising, giving examples of my everyday parenting strategies that I thought had not been helpful. I admitted that I had been critical in my attempts to correct them and I had been angry and shouted in the process. I acknowledged that although my intention was 'right' I recognise that they were hurt by my actions. I admitted my responsibility and my intention to do things differently. I asked them to forgive me and to give me the opportunity, and to help me on my journey of apprenticeship. Mind you, I did not exactly say apprenticeship to them. I was honest with them to tell them that I was learning and that I was asking them to be patient with me too. Then I had to forgive myself too.

I must say that when both parents make the decision to embark on the journey, I think the process may be relatively easier and the progress may be much more enjoyable. It is important however for you to be working together and consistently. If you are a single parent then do it because you can! It is considerably harder when your husband, wife or partner is not on the journey with you and you live together under the same roof, as it was in my case. Similarly, you might not be living in the same household but your partner who is not on the journey with you might have access to the children and that could make it harder too. But regardless of the challenges, it is always worthwhile to give it your best shot.

A little after a year into the journey, I decided to take time off work to give my time fully to my children. The apprenticeship so far had empowered me to realise that my teenagers needed more of me. I felt that I would struggle financially if I did not work but it came to a time when the money did not matter to me anymore. All I could see was that, I would lose my children to the world if I didn't invest more time into the apprenticeship. It felt like losing a job, however the difference was, this job is one that I cannot afford to lose because I cannot apply for another. Or better still, I am in it for life. Full stop. Secondly, I valued the relationship with my children more. All things happen for a reason. I injured my back, so I took time off work, however I did not return to work when I recovered. My husband, (now my ex-husband) was not in favour of me taking time off work but I felt it was necessary and nothing was going to stop me because I knew the vision, I had in my mind for the relationship I wanted between my children and I. I decided to prioritise my children over my career. I spent all my savings to meet my quota of household bills and responsibilities.

From March to September, 2018, I stayed home full time for the children. I served them. I performed intentional acts of service and quality time. I did the errands for them, more time to drop and collect to and from school. My daughter's friend used to give her lifts to school. I started offering to take her and by the time I realised she was requesting me to take her. How fulfilling, it felt good; I realised that she was actually enjoying my service and time. I actually gave them my time; I intentionally made myself available and I was conscious of it; spending quality time, doing things with them and for them, that communicated love to them. I remember I made them hot breakfast in the mornings, and their favourite was pancakes. For two years they enjoyed my pancakes. Today, my son is still a lover of my pancakes whereas my daughter does not like pancakes as much. I made time to spend one to one time with each of them and also together. I recall taking my daughter to a hotel for an overnight stay to relax her as she had a lot on her mind, which was a good experience although she was not very forth-coming. I did not take it personally, because I knew that the relationship was not great at the time. I was grateful that she agreed to come with me. I promised my son a similar experience as he was keen for it and he had an amazing time. We stayed in a hotel. I enjoyed myself too.

Then in October 2018, I started work again. For the first time I worked differently. I had resigned from my job; I did not have a permanent contract; I still do not have a permanent contract at the time of writing this book. I joined an agency, just to pay bills. Sometimes I went two weeks and sometimes even a whole month without working. So, I worked when I had spare time. It used to be the other way around: I would spend time with the children when I had spare time. It sounds horrible thinking about it now. It was so easy to give the leftover of me to my children without even realising it. It becomes part of you and it becomes 'normal' because everyone is doing it. It sounds weird talking about it and sharing this with you. But it is the truth. I feel now that it was an unfortunate situation: I used to give my children the spare time; spare of me; and spare energy whilst I gave the better part of me chasing money and career.

Within two years into my journey, my mindset had changed, I didn't have money at the bank like I used to, but I was a lot more content with my teenagers and my life. My priority was and is still is my apprenticeship career. Now that I don't have much money, I don't even stress about money. It probably sounds difficult to understand but that's the truth and a blessing. I have learned a lot and continue to learn to make necessary changes to my life and grow in my apprenticeship career. I can assure you that it's not easy but you can do it too. Just set your priorities and take the step into becoming intentional and look at your apprenticeship career from a different perspective. Become a committed apprentice and be led by the best.

Allow your Supervisor, the Holy Spirit, to work on your mindset.

'I am the Lord your God, who teaches you to profit, who leads you by the way you should go.' – Isaiah 48:17

Chapter 8

Lesson 5: Patience

You have to be able to wait long enough to develop and grow yourself to use the new strategies; be consistent in the application of those strategies and to wait for the progress. Be patient with yourself and be patient with your teenagers. Patience they say is a virtue but many lack this virtue. I think it is a character that needs cultivating and growing. A parent who is embarking on intentional nurturing needs loads and loads of patience. Especially if you are dealing with 'too late syndrome'. I required tons and tons of patience. I have grown in endurance and I am growing in long suffering. This requires extra supernatural power. I can only obtain this through the Holy Spirit, my Supervisor. Patience is one of the fruits of the Spirit. As parents, we are required to cultivate:

- Patience to be able to communicate
- Patience to understand our teenagers taking into account their developmental age and development stage.

To communicate means to talk understandably and with our teenagers. Remember **with** teenager not to or at your teenager. Most of us, if not all, are guilty of this: talking at our children. Situations arise where emotions are high, ego of being the 'adult' and parent factors in and the results are shouting and talking at our children. Forcibly and or demanding things from them that we possibly do not have ourselves. Patience requires a life-long learning attitude, that is why I have already said that be patient with yourself and your teenager. I am still learning and cultivating this virtue in different dimensions every day. Your children and teenagers or even your relationships or circumstances will challenge you: from patience, to endurance to long suffering. Yes! When you pursue intentional nurturing, that is, when you start to implement new strategies, you need to be patient for progress, and ultimately, the results. It means you need to be able to wait long enough to see the results that are the rewards. This meant that I had to work on my own character and inner self. The level and amount of patience required before you may begin to see some results depends on the kind of relationship you have; the degree of estrangement of the relationship, the age and developmental stage of the teenager, commitment and consistency.

Don't be too hard on yourself, stay calm, I know it's not easy, but most importantly, have a positive mindset so that you may be able to recognise the subtle changes that you might otherwise over look because you are too busy focusing on a big change or what is not going well: Negativity. I would encourage you to go out of your way to compliment your teenagers on the things they do well and lay off on the things they don't do so well. I am encouraging you to start today if you have not already been doing that. Show appreciation and appreciate them. They learn from you. That is why I share with all the mothers and parents I encounter on my journey of sharing my story, that the changes are yours to make not your teenagers. I am only sharing with you what works because it has worked for me. Start making the changes in yourself and then you will begin to see the impact on your teenagers when you wait long enough, when you are patient enough to see the fruits thereof. It is not a quick fix. So, if you are looking for a quick fix, I am sorry to tell you that this book might not help you. It is not a quick fix because I am sharing things with you that tackle the roots of behaviours and problems. The behaviours are just symptoms of an underlying cause. The Holy Spirit has taught me to tackle roots because the results thereof are longer lasting. I can only share what has worked for me. Be patient and relax and stay calm in the process. It is a journey. Renewing my mindset is the work of the Holy Spirit. He taught me. You won't be able to achieve it on your own strength. You may try but it would not be long lasting. It would not have the peace and the joy elements of it. It is just the truth. So, take your apprenticeship seriously.

I have made progress now, oh yes real progress! I am constantly learning and being consistent with the strategies that I implement. Remember I started my apprenticeship when my daughter was 15+ years and my son was around 9 years old. That was pretty late but not too late, because better late than never. Pretty late because things had hit rock bottom with my daughter. Although I was aware that my son and daughter have different personalities and temperament, it was possible that he might also turn out to be resentful towards us, his parents if things did not change for the better. I was so eager to embark on the new journey with or without my husband. Believe me it was difficult doing it on my own, not because I was a single parent, but because whenever I made progress with my daughter, my husband's 'old parenting strategies' sabotage the progress. I must make it clear that although the 'old parenting style' was not working, he was adamant about doing anything different. So that if I was doing one thing, he would also be doing another in the same household. That was tough. Not working as a team and the differences were confusing for the children because of the inconsistences.

I have learned the importance of patience on my new apprenticeship career and I am blessed with a renewed mindset. Consequently, I could see even the slightest positive progress which resulted in a change in behaviour or response due to the new strategies of nurturing. These slight positive changes motivated and fuelled my energy to continue with the career. Although there was no monetary renumeration, I was filled with hope and joy from the slightest positive responses that I was blessed to see from time to time. I can tell you it was fulfilling. Now, this is what I call tackling things from the roots. When you tackle issues or problems from the roots, that is the source, then the leaves (behaviour or symptom) so-to-speak as it would be in a tree, will change for the better. When a tree is withering, it is unwise to put the water and manure on the leaves; you put it to the roots. And then the trunk absorbs it and then the good stuff manifests in the leaves. It is the same with behaviour in ourselves or our teenagers or anybody else.

Let me share with you a typical example. You know how you ask your teenager to do something and you find yourself repeating the same thing over and over again because he or she does not do what you are asking? Over time as your teenager's behaviour continues, you become frustrated and angry and even feel disrespected. Consequently, you find yourself throwing more words at him or her in anger and when anger sets in voices become raised and you lose your cool. By the time you could say another word, your teenager is defending him or herself in the same words and volume and tone as yours. The inevitable is happening, that is shouting at each other. It's a battle. And the end of the day you as a parent feels disrespected and guess what, your teenager also feels disrespected too. I bet you would be wondering, "Why is my teenager feeling disrespected?" Your teenager feels disrespected because he/she feels that you have attacked him/her as a person. The point is not about the legitimacy of his or her feelings. The truth is, he or she is entitled to his or her feelings. Guess what, at that moment your teenager may decide to do what you are asking him or her to do. This may make you feel that shouting or arguing has given you results. However, the very behaviour that is frustrating for you does not go away; it emerges the next day or the day after only for you to find you and your teenager in the same battle ground again. Tell you what, I have been here as a mother and it is not nice, it is frustrating, exhausting, stressful and unfulfilling. Through learning to be intentional and learning from the best, I have learned a new way. And this is what I do.

My daughter was leaving the bathroom in a mess without tidying up after herself whenever she had her shower. I have learned to communicate with my teenagers in a way that is non-threatening. I said to her, "I would appreciate it and it would be nice if you would tidy up after yourself when you finished your shower." Then I would go and tidy up myself. Then she would do it again the next time she had her shower. I would also go to her and say the same thing to her. I had intentionally prepared myself that I was not going to be angry or frustrated, because this was a potential situation to get my blood boiling or anyone's blood boiling. This happened for a few times and each time I went to her. I pray a lot for my teenagers and myself and the way I nurture them as a committed apprentice. Then the Holy spirit reminded me of Isaiah 30:15:

"In quietness and confidence shall be your strength."

I understood that I was being directed to be quiet about it. Save my breath from throwing words at the problem. Simply, just keep quiet! Talking is only making the situation worse because it empowers it and is not solving anything. I had a couple of choices at least, to either keep doing what I was doing or choose to listen to the direction I was given by the Holy Spirit. I did the latter. I stopped going to her with my speech. What I did instead was I cleaned up after her each time without saying anything to her. I cleaned up because I like the place to be tidy. Thank God, I have legs and arms. Some of you might be thinking that I was encouraging laziness and irresponsibility. The answer is No! I was enlightened to not focus on the problem but rather focus on getting to the solution. My daughter knew what it meant to be considerate and caring and it was a matter of giving her the opportunity to decide to do that herself without me telling or prompting her. I was consistent and patient with this. Whilst I was focusing on the solution, I had to endure the situation for quite some time. This is what I call moving from patience to endurance.

Then one day, I walked into the bathroom after she had her shower, thinking I was going to clean up because I like to keep the place clean. To my amazement, the place was cleaned. I just looked in the mirror and smiled, and said "Thank you Lord!" I immediately went to her room to show appreciation to her for her effort at being considerate. Now, she cleans after herself most times, but when she does not do it, I clean up and I do it joyfully because I am doing it unto the Lord (Colossians 3:23). Serving your children and others is doing it onto the Lord. Knowing this, I am not frustrated, I am not stressed and I am not angry and my blood is stable, warm at 37 degrees Celsius not boiling hot at 100 degrees Celsius and over. This is what I call harmonising the spirit, soul and body. As a mother whenever something is not going well, I may bring the issue up with my children, maybe a couple of times after that I reflect on "in quietness and confidence shall be your strength." There are other times that I may not even say anything at all, but I put my trust in the Lord for making me a capable mother. It's so peaceful and fulfilling and I would want every mother and parent to experience this. I challenge you to give it a go. Try it!

I have gained so much experience and I have learned so much that I am able to share the stories of my journey with you. I am blessed to share that my relationship with my daughter has improved and continue to head in the right direction. Oh! don't get me wrong we still have some tough days but we are both learning and moving away from 'too late syndrome'. She sees that I am learning and she follows suit. I get through to my daughter better than I used to. She sometimes lets me into her world when she shares some of her feelings and thoughts with me; or what might be going on in her friendship group. I tell you some of the things are great to hear, whilst others could be mind-blowing and scary but I have learned to listen, not to be judgmental, not to begin with corrections of her behaviour and thoughts or that of her friends. I have learned to be appreciative whenever she shares, sometimes she may ask for my opinion other times I may give my opinion when she accepts the offer. It is important to me and to her to be involved in her world so that I can understand and have insight so that I can guide her appropriately when the opportunity arises. I am sharing with you today that the Holy Spirit has taught me how to overcome fear and trust in the truth to empower me to nurture my teenagers without physically forcing them or making them or demanding them to do the right thing. I will talk about fear in the lesson 8. I am really grateful for all that she shares with me. I could have been in the dark and become insignificant in her life; I could have lost my guidance role and lost my daughter to the world. I consider this rewarding and job satisfaction. We are moving from strength to strength. My daughter is almost 20 years old and I can say that I have my daughter. I can say with most certainty that I would have lost my daughter if I had not changed the 'everyday parenting'; and the 'leave-to-chance parenting' to intentional nurturing.

It pays to be patient; and consistency is very important in the implementing any new strategy. Take this from a children's Nurse, a health visitor by profession and a mother who has been through it. I am blessed to be able to share this with you because I have been through all this and it would be a shame to keep this my story to myself. I find it worthwhile to be able to share my story...my truth!

I encourage you to choose to become an intentional nurturer.

'In quietness and confidence shall be your strength.' – Psalm 30:15

Chapter 9

Lesson 6: Consistency

Consider these key words and ponder over them as you read this lesson. Then reflect and see how it relates to the other lessons. Also, think about how you can relate to these:

- Determined
- Positive or positivity
- Persevere or perseverance
- Initiative
- Focus

When it comes to nurturing, contradictory and confusing strategies are no nos. Consistency is simply doing the right thing without giving up for as long as it takes till you see progress - that is what you call consistency.

I have learned over the journey and the career of parenting apprenticeship to be consistent in my approach to intentional nurturing. From where I started my apprenticeship career, taking into account the state of the relationships in the home environment, at the fact that I was the only parent on the journey, I needed to be consistent buttered with patience. I can assure you that I did get it wrong sometimes but I was determined enough to start again, making changes where necessary. But I did not lose sight of what I wanted to achieve. I focused on the solution and not the problem.

I used to ignore my daughter for few hours or a couple of days, not speaking to her when I thought she was rude (this was a learned behaviour). I did this thinking that she would come and apologise, which rarely happened. When I commenced my apprenticeship, I was taught that ignoring my daughter was a wrong approach. Ignoring my daughter was not nurturing, full stop. I was enlightened to take the initiative to speak with her and discipline her when appropriate. Discipline here is not about talking at my daughter or giving her a dressing down or implementing harsher boundaries or giving her a time out in the naughty corner. It just means enforcing the boundaries that we have discussed and agreed upon as fair. I would go out of my way to do things for her and be there for her as a mother would, without depriving her of any motherly love. I would break the tension and seek to make peace by speaking with her or do something for her, or say something nice to her and then I would seek to discuss the incident as appropriate. Of course, at first, she did not want to hear it or know. She was still head-hard, holding grudges and did not want to care. This went on for a while. If you would remember from the lesson one, if you want your child to do something, then you as the parent have to take the initiative with your actions to model it for the child. Besides, she was used to my old attitude of ignoring her so to change that attitude requires patience and time and of course consistency in my new change in my attitude towards her. I was not discouraged because I was focused and determined. At times it was so difficult that I would cry, not in front of her of course, but I persevered and the comforter, the Holy Spirit was right there with me in those moments. Once I finished crying and taking comfort from my Supervisor, I was good to go again.

I can confidently say that I put conscious time, effort, and my energy into nurturing my teenagers and I have learned and continuously learn to be consistent with it. I would not achieve this having another full-time 9-5 job. This is a full-time job with overtime! I was dedicated, I learned to increase the words of affirmation, words of encouragement and to show appreciation to the young person she had become. I recognised her talents and I highlighted them. I was available to my daughter and my son to drop them to school and collect them from school, make them breakfast. I started writing them notes, or letters with encouraging and loving words. My son took to these very well but my daughter was a hard nut. I didn't blame her. She was older and as such she was more of a challenge. The trust between us was broken. She did not trust me. I was keen to rebuild the trust, and oh boy, I had worked for that trust.

Then suddenly, I realised that she was enjoying the fact that I was available to her and her brother. She would request pancakes in the mornings. So did her brother. She then also started requesting to be dropped off at school and be collected. She would ask me to collect her from school even when her friend offered to give her a lift. She preferred me to collect her. I knew something was working. I also had to learn new ways of communicating with her. I remember one time, I had a conversation with her concerning her behaviour one morning before school, she was actually quiet, then when she returned from school, she apologised. She actually said, "I am sorry Mum, for this morning." I was elated. My approach was yielding results – as I was consistent with my intentional nurturing. As I have mentioned before, the responses from her were subtle and seldom, nevertheless present. I was blessed with the eyes to see these positive changes in her attitude and behaviour. The challenging thing was the inconsistency in her behaviour. I mean that when I saw something positive from her behaviour, the next minute she would be doing something so heart-breaking and would be back into the 'I don't care, whatever' mode. She in fact said it over and over again, "I don't care." Even then, I continued in my approach.

Then I realised that there were differences between her attitude towards me and her attitude towards her father. She would respond better to me compared to her father. I remember one time, she asked me to drop her off at school, but her father offered to do this when he heard her asking me. She refused saying that, she would rather walk the distance to school. And it was raining that day. That was how bad the relationship between my daughter and her father was. And I bet you anything that it would have been the same with me, had I not become a committed apprentice.

When I realised that her response to me was better compared to her attitude towards her father, I encouraged her father to apply some of the strategies I was using for nurturing. He was still reluctant. What he did was rather find ways to highlight that the strategies were not working. So, on days that were 'not-so-good' in regards to my daughter's attitude, my husband would emphasise that things were not working as well as I was making them out to be. What he did not understand was the fact that I completely understood and expected some days to be 'not-so-good' because of where the relationship had begun from and where it was going. Every road to change has 'potholes and bumps' on the road. So that the 'not-so-good' days or moments were not deterrents but rather I used them as encouragement to persevere with consistency. So, whenever he came up with these negativities, I could see past them to the bigger picture. I admitted that the 'not-so-good' moments were expectedly a lot initially, but I could also see the positives in every situation and would highlight them to myself to make them real and tangible. Over time the positives became so vivid to me. In the past I would have focused on the negatives and lost sight of the positives even when there were more to celebrate than criticise. So that the whole experience would go down as negative. If you are not careful, as a parent you might feel that you need to correct or highlight every single error in judgement or something that your teenager does wrong. But I have learned through being a committed apprentice that I don't have to. I have learned to celebrate the good deeds all the time and to constructively discuss only the necessary concerning behaviours, deeds or attitudes. I have learned to be selective.

With this change of mindset, I became more understanding of situations and I learned not to take things so personally. The more I highlighted the positives and paid less attention to the shortfalls (not that I was in denial, but I was not afraid of them like I used to be) the more my consistency soared, less lectures on criticisms, less stressed we both were. I was determined to do more. As I continued to see her response to me and the direction of our relationship, I became convinced that I was doing the right thing. That was satisfying. I realised that I was becoming competent in my approach and that was reflected in my confidence. This was also growth for me.

Thinking back to the times when the relationship was so poor that my daughter was unhappy at home, she stopped inviting her friends over to our house. She used to invite friends over when she was younger, it was a delight that on her 17th birthday a few of her friends came over to the house to get ready for her birthday dinner that she had organised for herself and friends. She said to me that she did not want us, her parents involved. This was a year and half into intentional parenting. I realised and understood that she had lost trust in us, her parents. I could recollect another episode when she was about 15 years old, she said to me that she was only living at home because of her little brother. It was no surprise that when she found a part time job when she was 16 years, she put her little brother, her 9-year-old brother down as her next of kin. I was blessed and fortunate that she opens up and drops some of what I call 'gold nuggets' or 'bombshells' depending on how you look at it. When she made that statement when she was 15 years old, I was not a committed apprentice then, I did not think much of it at the time, although I felt that she was being ungrateful for saying something like that. So, the statement was viewed as a 'bombshell.' When I decided to view my parenting apprenticeship career from another perspective, I viewed such utterances as 'gold nuggets'. With a changed mindset I had learned not to take them personally. I considered myself blessed to be given the opportunities to gain insight into her thoughts and feelings. I could understand from her statements how hurt she was and the fact that she had lost trust in us was clearer to me. It was heart-breaking for me that my teenager was feeling this hurt to the point that she had even thought of leaving home but the good thing was that she cared enough to stay at home for her little brother.

Rebuilding trust is a difficult and tedious business. It requires forgiveness. You might not get the trust back although you might be forgiven. It requires the ingredients of patience and consistency, the appropriate mindset, and the willingness to work for it. I remember that when my daughter was responding better to me, my husband was of the opinion that the approach was not working however he admitted to the fact that she responded better to me. Now how was that? I encouraged him to use some of the strategies which he tried sometimes. However, he could not be patient or cultivate the mindset to be consistent with it, so he gave up. I guess what I am really saying is that I wanted my ex-husband and I to be on the journey together because we are their parents. What I have learned is that some people will choose never to be ready to embark on intentional nurturing especially when the relationships have gone downhill. It might be due to their own personal insecurities which they may or may not be aware of. They might say, "It's too difficult" or they might feel that it is the responsibility of their maturing adults or adult children to make the effort to change or reach out. For such people with such excuses no one can help them until they are ready to help themselves. I believe everyone can change if they want to, and everyone has a choice no matter what the situation. I know people sometimes rationalise their behaviours and choices by saying, "I had no choice". I think that is not true. As long as you have options or have to decide between two things you have a choice. For example, I can choose to tell the truth or lie. I can decide to eat yam or sweet potatoes. Sometimes we look at the severity of the consequence and convince ourselves that we have no choice. Well, I will leave this with you to ponder over to see what you believe.

Doing the apprenticeship journey on my own with the occasional in and out of my husband made it difficult to say the least, due to the inconsistencies. Therefore, I decided to concentrate on what I was doing and to be consistent with it and leave my husband out of it; especially with regards to our daughter. Our son was younger and he seemed compliant with things which made it seem easier with him. As a result, my husband felt comfortable with his parenting of him. Now 'leaving him out of it' does not work, especially when we all lived in the same household, because the inconsistences in strategies still existed. These inconsistences in nurturing strategies between the parents created knock back effects which affected the progress that I had made with my daughter. When it did happen, I had to pick up the pieces which made it extremely difficult. But I continued. Sometimes I cried and cried and cried some more, I felt so drained and felt so alone because not only was I nurturing my teenagers, I had to sort out the emotional upheaval between my daughter and her father from their battles and personality clashes. They are both strong-willed. Sometimes the arguments and tension in the house was not good for anyone, especially the children. The Holy Spirit kept me going as I battled spiritually and physically. I became hopeful and my soul was peaceful.

Until one day, on the 3rd of September 2018, my children and I found ourselves moving out of our home. I think it was actually a house at that point although we thought of it as a home. I hope you do know that a house is different from a home. That was the beginning of my separation from my husband and eventual divorce. I am delighted to be a committed apprentice and I am still in the business of intentional nurturing. My relationship with my daughter and son is flourishing. What a delight!

I put on the armour of God and I battle as a committed apprentice. So can you!

'...put on the whole armour of God, that you may be able to stand against the wiles of the devil. For not wrestle against flesh and blood, but against principalities, against powers, against the rulers of darkness of this age, against spiritual hosts of wickedness in the heavenly places.' – Ephesians 6:10-12

Chapter 10

Lesson 7: Competent and Confidence

I used to be so furious and upset when I wanted to speak to my daughter and she said she did not want to talk. How could she not want to talk? How she could just watch me talk and decides to ignore me? I couldn't accept that. I used to want to 'make her talk'. I would be in her space and keep 'nagging' her about what's wrong, talk to me, blah blah blah. I did not quite understand why and how she wouldn't open up to me, her mother. Sometimes, she would either remain quiet or she would explode angrily with lots of harsh words and I would react in an inappropriate manner. No wonder she didn't want to speak. In the end her emotions and mine would be all over the place; flying around in mid-air, bouncing off the furniture and eventually disappearing into thin air. Although my aim was to help and be there for my her, it always turned out very disastrous.

Other times whilst she was talking, I might interrupt and seek to correct her feelings or ways, offering solutions which I thought I should be doing as her mother. It is important to point out that when I busied myself looking for solutions, I was not actually listening to her because I had anticipated what she was saying and had drawn conclusions. I could be wrong because I did not give myself the opportunity to actually hear her feelings from her words and to empathise. Little did I know that I was communicating wrongly to her. I was in fact infringing on her independence and 'trying to fix things' or 'still trying to fix her', because I would be thinking, I am her parent and the adult and as such, I had to give her all the solutions and even 'show' her how to feel. Again, no wonder she did not want to talk. She soon put me in the category, 'You don't understand'. She also felt that I didn't listen, so what was the point? And when teenagers and even younger ones feel that you don't listen to them, they feel that whatever they say does not matter and most importantly they do not matter to you. In fact, it is human nature to feel that way. So then, she eventually decided to close off and 'shut down'. Now, 'shutting down' was something she could control knowingly or unknowingly to hurt me and or make herself feel better. This is called passive aggressive.

I had to learn a different way when I started intentional nurturing. The lessons were flowing in and I was hungry for them. I was taking everything in. Being intentional meant that I had to be conscious of everything and that meant that I began reflecting in a meaningful way. And in no time my reflection skill was sharpened. This progressed quite quickly. I still reflect quite a lot because that is one way that I communicate with the Holy Spirit. I started journaling too as part of my reflection process. It was amazing! I never used to journal until I became a committed apprentice and now, I cannot stop. Honestly, I do not want to stop!

Welcome to the lesson of respect. As I have said before, Jesus respects me so He knocks and waits for my response. I learned to respect my daughter when she said she was not ready to speak. I had to keep to it, be consistent with it, to let her know and understand that she could trust me to respect her choices and feelings. I had to build her trust in me on that level. I would go to her room and as soon as I asked her once and I realised that the response was unwelcoming or I was greeted with silence, I would leave her alone. As I kept doing this, my observation and listening skills developed to pick up even her non-verbal cues. I was in tune with them. I was amazed how I was developing personally. I could actually be patient enough to wait till she was ready. Sometimes as soon as she heard my footsteps, she would close or shut her bedroom door, then I knew that she was telling me to leave her alone. I also saw that when she was ready for me, she would open her door.

It is important to respect our children and our teenagers. More often than not, we get back what we give. It means that when we give respect to our children, they give it back to us. Our teenagers expect us to respect their opinions and feelings too. And most importantly they expect us to respect them as people and individuals in their own rights as human beings. Remember from the lesson on *unlearn and relearn* that when we want something from our children or want them to do something, we as their parents, leaders and role models have to do it first by developing that character within ourselves. I once read this "How can I command respect when no one respects my command?" The response was, "Maybe you need to stop commanding respect and start respecting respect?"

My listening skills evolved to a whole new level and I could actually 'hear' the root of her concerns and her frustrations and her 'cry for help' in the midst of raining her words in anger. I was always appreciative of her 'shouting' her concerns because first of all she had opened out and that was when and how I could actually identify the root of her anger and how best to support her. It is much better for our teenagers to be talking, regardless of what they say and how they deliver it than for them to 'shut down'. I usually would find an appropriate time when I would speak with her regarding a concern I might have picked up during her raining of words and would ask her to elaborate on it. Prior to becoming a committed apprentice, I used to hear a rude, disobedient and ungrateful child with an attitude speaking. I would be so angry and frustrated that I would let her go a couple of days without her feeling my motherly love. I feel even uncomfortable and embarrassed now that I am sharing this with you. I am glad things are different now.

I remember that one day my daughter asked to spend the night at her best friend's home, which I agreed. It turned out that, it was not true. She was in fact going to a house party at a male friend's home where she would also spend the night. I must say that I was blessed that I always found out when she told a lie; at least the important ones anyways. That day I had spare time so I went to work as my daughter was out of home at her part time retail job and going to her friend's after work. My son had gone to spend time with his father. My husband and I had separated at the time. It was a long day at work (12-hour shift) so when I finished work around 8pm, I called her over the telephone to make sure that she arrived okay at her friend's. I had previously sent her a text to inform her that I would call her after work. I could not get through on her phone, so I called her friend. To my amazement it turned out she was somewhere else. I eventually got through to her on her phone and she informed me where she was. I hope you can imagine what I did. Of course, I went straight there to get her. I travelled miles and miles on lonely the dark roads and got to her at nearly 11pm We arrived home around midnight. You can imagine how exhausted I was but in all I was grateful that my daughter was safe and being exhausted didn't even matter.

Before we started the journey back home, she apologised for her behaviour, then I said what I wanted to say and explained to her about being honest with me. However, she became upset and angry and her rain started pouring down. I was quiet the whole time she was 'raining' then suddenly, I heard "I lied because you don't let me do anything so I had to tell you I was going to my best friend because I knew you would not object to that..." I kept calm and waited for her to finish. Once she had finished, there was a long pause, we were still in the car at this time; the car was stationary; still parked along the roadside near her friend's. I then said her sentence back to her, "I lied to you because you don't let me do anything, so I had to tell you I was going to my best friend because I knew you would not object to that..." and I asked her to elaborate on that. She did open up to elaborate and we had a conversation. In my mind I did 'allow her to do things', but it's obvious that she had a different take on that. I considered her words carefully and analytically and came to the conclusion that I might have been a little over protective in some aspects to some extent. We came to an agreement. Being honest and being truthful means a lot to me and I would like my children to trust me so I have to learn to trust her first. You would remember from lesson one when I talked about role modelling and leading for your children to follow. If she believed that I trusted her she would tell me the truth no matter what and she would believe I would be able to handle it because I trusted her to do the right thing. So, if my actions were to some extent contributing to my daughter's being untruthful then I was prepared to evaluate my actions. Let me highlight this: it was not easy to trust her when she had been lying to me. I struggled with it but eventually, I got better and better at it because I put my trust in God instead. I do know that she lies occasionally, especially when whatever she was into was new and had not yet shared it with me. Otherwise, she tells me exactly, where is she going and what she is doing whether I approve or not. The Holy Spirit gave a lesson on fear and trust which enabled me to focus on God not my daughter.

So, you see I am constantly learning and putting into action what I learn. Life after all is a lifelong learning process. You can choose to learn and grow or choose to be stagnant. And there was no point not practising what I learn. It's better if I didn't learn and claim ignorance. But remember actions which include decisions and choices whether you are ignorant of them or not, have consequences.

I have understood what being consistent with the strategies and being patient, have demonstrated over time, I have become competent and confident in the intentional nurturing of my teenagers. I have also demonstrated growth through cultivating and developing my own character. I appreciated that I was learning so much more from teenagers than I used to. I have learned to be confident in the direction of the Holy Spirit and I have become better and better at recognising the 'still small voice of the Holy Spirit'. The age gap between my children is wide so the different developmental stages meant that some of the things that my son might respond to would not necessarily be appreciated by my daughter who is almost 7 years older than my son. It was tough and emotionally draining especially at the beginning because of all the hard, conscious work that had to be invested in order to undo all the wrong things before new things could be imparted. I however embraced the challenge because I actually enjoyed and appreciated the positive changes in my own character.

I do appreciate that we all learn at different rates and that means that putting things into practice might be a different ball game because we are all different. I also know that not everyone would even choose to actually practise what they learn. We are different; however, I am almost certain that you can do it if you want and choose to. The truth is as parents, we are commissioned:

'Do not to provoke your children to wrath, but bring them up in the training and admonition of the Lord.' – Ephesians 6:4

Chapter 11

Lesson 8: Fear

Fear! Fear! Fear!

I have never looked at 'fear' the way I look at fear now. I have come to the realisation that the way I felt and behaved and acted was more often than not due to fear. Most of us do not realise that fear is the foundation of a lot of our actions and behaviour. Let me give you a typical example. We tell lies because we are afraid of the consequences. As a result, we go on to tell more lies to protect the previous lie. By the time we come to our senses or caught in our lies, we have entangled ourselves in lies and ultimately have to face the dreaded consequence only to realise that it is a lot worse.

How fear undermined my parenting, making me achieve the opposite of what I wanted to achieve.

- My ex-husband and I were critical in our parenting of our daughter because we were afraid that if our child did not correct her mistakes, she wound not make it in life. Mind you, I did not comprehend at the time that fear was the root of our behaviour. I am not saying that correction of mistakes means that you are afraid. What I am saying is that when fear underpins your reasoning (most of the time you are unaware), your actions and behaviour are affected adversely. So, then all our attention and focus were geared at pointing out her faults and everything she did not do right. As if that was not enough, we put pressure on her to make her pay attention to those mistakes and faults.

- Then we feared that if we did not put enough pressure on her to notice and acknowledge her mistakes and correct them, she would fail in the world. Then of course as we busied ourselves with her faults, we lost sight of the things she did so well and her achievements.

- My daughter's father was also particularly critical of her style of learning and the subjects she seemed to be more interested in. She was very much interested in drama, playing her guitar and piano and singing. These are her talents. In fact, she is good and performs amazingly. The problem was that her father did not place value on those subjects – he said that those subjects would not take her anywhere (fear of not going to be success-ful). To him she had to spend her time studying the subjects he considered 'important'. This created a lot of tension in the household between my daughter and her father with me trying to diffuse the situation. I thought this was sad and I tried to give him insight into various styles of learning. I for instance, I shared with him that I do not like to learn in a totally silent environment, so I prefer to have the television on or have mu-sic on in the background whilst studying. Our daughter studies with music either on the background or with her earphones. He could not accept this, to him studying in this manner meant that she was not taking her studies seriously.

The sad thing was that the more pressure we put on her, the more she made mistakes. We became angry each time with each mistake and she became fearful and timid, putting more stress on herself to do better. In the end I believe she came to the conclusion that we did not love her nor care about her. In her mind, no matter what she did we had something bad to say about it. Until she did not care anymore. This contention was not limited to studies alone, it spilt into all areas of our lives.

I remember an incident that happened between my daughter and her father. I had to take my daughter outside of the house to control the situation. She broke down telling me, "I do not know what to do with my life, I try so hard to do the right thing but I end up making mistakes and doing the wrong things. I do not like my life and I wish I was dead." This broke my heart. I had commenced my apprenticeship at the time and I had changed my nurturing strategies. The relationship between my daughter and I was not great but I could say that she responded better to me than her father. I thought it had something to do with the fact that I had resorted to doing things differently. I was glad that she opened up to share her thoughts and feelings with me that day which gave me insight into how to support her. This is just by the way. The point I want to make is that, parenting underpinned with fear destroys our teenagers' self-worth and confidence rather building self-belief.

- When my daughter's father and I felt that we could not get my daughter to comply as she used to, I think, we became afraid that this meant she wouldn't respect us and had become disobedient. As a result, we turned the volume of our voices up. (This I have now learned, is manipulation). Then she also learned to turn her volume up. The more we shouted, she shouted back with resistance. Soon enough, we were all shouting at each other, leaving us emotionally drained and unloved. We as parents felt angry because we considered her to be ungrateful and unappreciative, whilst I believe she felt unloved and uncared for. That was fear controlling us. A lesson well learnt.

- Fear can make us overly protective of our children to the extent that our children may feel suffocated. Taking into account the age and developmental stage of the child, some children may resort (especially the teenagers) to telling lies to free themselves from the suffocation. Others stay put under their parents' overly protective wings and thereby lacking the experience that comes with growing up into independent adults. Whilst others engage in risk taking behaviours the moment they taste 'freedom' from the overly protective wings of their parents. I am not implying that all children lie because of suffocation from overly protective parents, what I am saying is that children in this category may go the extra mile to free themselves. Our fears may lead our children into the very things we want to protect them from.

My daughter resorted to telling lies about her where-abouts or where she was going. Each time I found out she would apologise only to repeat it again. She was 17 years, approaching 18 years at the time, and because she wanted to go out, she would lie to me, risking herself and leaving me in the dark. I reflected on this and I realised that fear had made me quite restrictive although I thought I was allowing her to do things. I learned that I was a little tensed about the fact that I didn't want anything to happen to her especially now that we lived separately from her father. I did not want him to have a reason to blame me with my new strategies. Therefore, fear crept in without me knowing and controlling my actions.

From fear to Faith

I came to acknowledge that I couldn't keep a tight grasp on her. I had to loosen up. I could loosen up and leave the rest that I could not control in the Creator's hands. That is the good thing about the apprenticeship. I had no reason to be anxious or fearful when I have the Omnipresent God who would protect her. His word tells me that:

> *'Be anxious for nothing, but with prayer and supplication, with thanks giving make your request known to God and the peace of God which transcends all understanding will guide your minds and hearts.' – Phil 4: 6-7*

So, I am saying that I was encouraged to overcome fear by doing what I have to do, by asking my Source, my Supernatural force, my God, to protect my daughter whenever she was out of my sight. I do the same for her younger brother. It is funny how we as parents think that we can protect our children when they are in our presence. The fact that we can see them in our presence gives us the reassurance that we can protect them. However, the truth is: it is God who protects them. If God allows anything (plans of the enemy) to befall them in our presence it would happen regardless of our proximity to them. I relented knowing that I had back-up and she became truthful and comfortable to some extent to keep me in the loop of her whereabouts. Believe me, some of the places, I didn't like and I wished she wouldn't go there, but I was comfortable knowing that Someone far bigger and greater who I trust, is watching over her. I say to the glorification of God that my fear was turned to faith. What I did was to pray and commit her into Jesus' hand and ask the Holy Spirit to be with her. Then I left it. I felt peaceful after that. I am less stressed, no arguments and no confrontation because I chose to be a committed apprentice. Amazing! So, you see why I have stressed earlier that as a parent you need a supernatural force to enable you to rise above fear through courage. I have learned to replace fear with faith to allow me to live and nurture my teenagers without the crippling effect from fear. I am not saying that I never get afraid. I do but the difference now is the fact that I am blessed to be conscious of it; blessed to have the knowledge of the antidote and blessed to be able to apply the antidote (faith in my God).

Amidst gun violence, reports of missing children, social media, gangs, sexual exploitation and grooming, and drugs, just to mention a few, of course parents have the tendency to over protect their children. Because we don't want our children to become what we see and hear around us – another statistic. The fear motivates our behaviour to become overprotective, restrictive or very stern/critical with our children to the extent that they rebel or become timid. I am not suggesting that correction of our teenagers is not appropriate, what I am driving at is the fact that when the correction is motivated by fear, it defeats the purpose. One of the important lessons I have been blessed to learn is the fact that I cannot live and nurture my teenagers in fear. Although my intentions may be positive, nurturing my teenagers in fear yields negative results for both myself and my teenagers. I am grateful for the information, knowledge, the lessons, and the change of mindset to transform my thinking and my thoughts to eliminate fear as part of being a committed apprentice.

Fear will emerge in different situations of our lives because we live in a broken world. God who purposed us to be parents knew this, so he has not 'given us the spirit of fear, but of power and of love and of a sound mind' (2 Timothy 1:7). He does not want us to be afraid, neither does he want us to nurture our children in fear. 'There is no fear in love; but perfect love casts out fear, because fear involves torment. But he who fears has not been made perfect in love' (1 John 4:16-18). Now the question is: "Are you parenting in fear?

'Fear not, for I have redeemed you; I have called you by your name; you are Mine. When you pass through the waters, I will be with you; and through the rivers, they shall not overflow you. When you walk through fire, you shall not be burned, nor the flame scorch you. For I am the Lord your God.' – Isaiah 43:1-2

Module 3:

INTENTIONALLY LOVING MY TEENAGERS.

I think it would be good to share some practical things that I learned to communicate love to my teenagers.

I love my teenagers, but do they feel and know my love? I can answer that question confidently today to say, "Yes!" My son knows and feels my love. My daughter knows and feels my love. I would ask you the same question toady: "Do your children and teenagers know and feel your love?" Please do not be quick to answer it; think about it. I am asking you to think about it because you might respond from your own perspective. I am asking you to consider it from their perspective. "Do your teenagers know and feel your love?". Before I became a committed apprentice, I thought I loved my children and that was enough. As long as I was there, being a 'mother' and working hard to obtain the financial means to provide their needs; I loved them and I thought they should know that. I felt that I was doing my best to love them so they must recognise that. In fact, if they thought otherwise, I would have thought and felt that they were ungrateful because I provided them with so much that I did not get as a child or teenager. In my mind I was communicating the message of love to my children by putting food on the table and putting clothes on their backs amongst other things but the question was, "did they receive the love message as I had intended?" When we communicate information, there is the sender of the information and the receiver of the information. It is important that the message is received and interpreted by the receiver as intended by the sender. I am trying to say that although my intention might have been love in whatever I was doing for my children, it was important that my children received the message of love as I had intended, otherwise there was miscommunication.

I turned to Dr Chapman's 5 Languages of Love, as I read the book, I was enlightened to comprehend that what I was doing was not being received as love. In fact, there were other parents in the book that were doing what I was doing and missing the mark; way off. As we miss the mark of communicating love to our teenagers over time, it has implications for the emotional and healthy wellbeing of our teenagers. According to Dr Chapman when our teenagers run on empty on their emotional love tanks it affects their entire lives in a way that their ability to navigate physically, emotionally, socially, intellectually and spiritually is all impaired. It was as if a light switch came on in my head. I could actually understand how I had ended up with 'an alien' in my home. I took the book seriously and reflected on the love languages.

The love languages are words of affirmation, gifts, acts of service, quality time and personal touch. A nurturing parent must learn to speak the primary language of each and every child and teenager in the family effectively for them to receive and feel loved. The same principle is also true for our marriage relationships and other intimate relationships. However, children and teenagers require a sprinkling of the rest of the love languages in order to thrive and build a strong emotional love that will enable them to thrive in the wider world. My work was cut out for me. I had to learn all five languages and speak them to my teenagers. I found myself having to learn 5 languages from out of the blue. Could you imagine learning to speak English, French, German, Latin and Mandarin? The good thing was I was already fluent in English so 4 languages to go. According to Chapman as individuals, we tend to be already fluent in our own love language. That is, we tend to communicate love to others in our own love languages, that is, the way we receive and interpret love. So, you could say that I had four languages to learn. But first I had to acknowledge my own love language. I am sharing this about me with you: I am like a teenager; I may have one primary language but I also love a sprinkling of the other four. My primary language is quality time fused with physical touch, served with acts of service and garnished with words of affirmation and gifts. Uh-huh! that is me! Anyways enough about me. I knew it was not going to be easy to learn and speak the languages fluently besides the 'too late syndrome' of my situation but I was determined to do my best; my utmost best under supervision! I learned to '...love in deed and in truth.' – John 3:18

Chapter 12

Lesson 9: Loving through words

Words can build and words can destroy.

Words can mould and words can unmould.

Words can put together and words can pull apart.

L oving through words is *words of affirmation*. It comes in three different categories. They are words of praise, words of affection and speaking the language in the presence of others.

I know that teenage years is a time and stage where teenagers are finding themselves and struggling with self-identity issues. They are constantly comparing with others to see how they measure up and more often than not they might come to the conclusion that they fall short of this or that. They feel bad about themselves wanting to fit in and measure up to their peers and others in their friendship groups. I must say that I have been a teenager once, however what our teenagers go through in our world today is on a different level due to the exposure to technology and social media. Loving through words by using words of affirmation is the way to help our teenagers in the struggle for self-identity and independence. Do you know what? This is also the stage that unfortunately, many parents, including me, increase the tap on negative words because we are struggling to get through to our teenagers. And why do we struggle? We struggle because we use the same strategies we used when our maturing adults were children and guess what? Our maturing adults do not respond to those strategies any longer. I turned up the negative words and wanting to correct every mistake of my daughter.

Words of praise

Words of praise is simply recognising and commending the accomplishment of the teenager. It is also important to point out specifics rather than generalisations. This is an important fact to learn when it comes to loving through words. It is simple but not easy. For when I was starting from a place that my attention had been on pointing out wrong things; to suddenly change to point out positives was not that easy. First, I had to accept that every teenager does something good. I had to accept that my daughter did some good things. Second, I had to change my mindset. I had to reset my mind. I had to tune my mind to be able to see and recognise the positives. I thought I must focus on what she did well and commend her on those. Now this is something that I always say to mothers and parents that I encounter when I talk about changing for growth. Parents usually want their teenagers' behaviour to change and so they expect the teenagers to just do the changes, however I say to them, we as parents have to change first. The changes we make in ourselves ultimately effect changes in them.

As I practised looking for positives and commending her, I moved from a negative attitude mother to a positive attitude mother. It was difficult at first, but I persevered and I had my Supervisor with me who encouraged me. I am blessed to say that within no time I could even see positives in even the worst of situations. I learned to actively and consciously examine to see the good even when things became very difficult. It was a miracle to be able to see this no matter how slight or little they were to commend my daughter. As I have already described my husband on the other hand, struggled to see any positives and even he would not acknowledge the ones that he saw as he considered them 'little and insignificant'. I recollect I used to point them out for him but he refused to see, let alone accept them. He would say that how come I was the only one that could see these so-called positives, he could not see them? Do you know the answer? That is a blessing that comes with becoming a committed apprentice because I was transformed by a renewal of the mind. Renewal of the mind has enabled me to see things that others don't. It is true and I want all mothers and parents, and anyone in a helping position to children and teenagers to be blessed with. Do you still need more convincing to became a committed apprentice? Continue to read.

In practical terms, for example, sometimes when I walked into my daughter's room that looked like a bomb site, however her bed had been made nicely, I then commented on how beautiful her bed looked. Again, she may eat and decide to wash her plate, I would commend her on that. The day that she decided to do the dishes for the whole family I would commend her, show my appreciation and highlight that it was helpful. I even commended her on the fact that she went to school every day. You might think it sounds crazy. But it is not, because at the time there were other parents whose teenagers were refusing to go to school or were truants. It was actually a blessing that she got up every day and went to school. At least regardless of whatever we were going through as a family, she still got up every morning to go to school. For me this was something good that required recognition. You would be surprised but there were other parents who were struggling and so would pay their teenagers to go to school and to do their school work.

Over time I shifted my attention from looking for 'perfection' according to my definition, to recognising effort. I remember one time I was in discussion with a parent who was having trouble with his son about inconsistencies in carrying out his household responsibilities. I suggested that he recognise and praise his son's efforts than look for perfection. He found that challenging because he said, "how could I reward laziness?" For him, when the task was not done to what he defined as 'perfection' each time, it was sheer laziness. I understood his position very well and I felt for him because that was where I had come from. That was my attitude when I was parenting and not nurturing. I explained to him that when you recognise and praise efforts, it has nothing to do with laziness. It is simply praising efforts. Over time the teenager in question would realise that he is pleasing his father and begin to do it consistently which will ultimately bring about progress in quality. Again, it is about timing. When the teenager realises that he is pleasing his parent and the parent is actually acknowledging that, the teenager would then be open to welcome instructions for improving quality. I was enlightened to grab that concept. Unfortunately, not everyone would grab it. I grabbed it because I decided to be a committed apprentice. I am hoping that you will too.

Even now that my daughter is nearly 20 years of age, I still do that. Sometimes she tidies up her whole room and I commend her. Other times, I may only commend her on her dressing table. That is ok. I know that I have taught her how to clean and tidy up her room. Now that she is a maturing adult, she can make that decision and choice for herself as a person to tidy up her room or not, whatever she decides to do, she has to deal with the consequences. I know that when she is out there, she cleans and tidies up like no one. I am not afraid that people would say, "Her mother did not do a good job at teaching her."

I have learned to go the extra mile to recognise the efforts of my teenagers. I went to watch my daughter's drama performance somewhere in London with her younger brother some time ago. It was a college performance. The play itself and its theme was over my head. My daughter had a small part in the whole piece, however I made sure that she knew and felt that I was proud of her. I laughed and cheered the loudest whenever she spoke. I mean the things that she was saying and how she said them were funny because others laughed as well but I made sure I was heard. And after the show, I was talking about it and happy and cheering her on. I even recited some of the words she said back to her. I could see that she was pleased. I praised her for her part well executed even if I did not get the whole story. That is what fills love tanks.

My daughter's primary love language appears to be gifts according to the results she achieved based on the questionnaire she completed to ascertain her love language. Consequently, I have given her meaningful gifts to speak love to her. I however, felt at the time that words of affirmation were useful too, especially as she has lost her confidence as a result of our (parents) use of negative words. I felt that her primary love language is words of affirmation. I still feel that way now because, I have seen the effect of the negative words and criticisms on her life. Even today after all the words of affirmation that she is showered with, she deals with anxiety and still puts pressure on herself to wanting to do everything right. She does not want to make a mistake.

And obviously as human beings we are prone to mistakes and she is no exception. So, that when something is highlighted for improvement, she still feels like she cannot do anything right. I remember once when an incident happened a couple of times at work and it was brought up, she made the comment whilst crying, "I feel like I cannot do anything right." However, she had done so well at her work and she received positive feedback and encouragement both from her employer and I. She then had further training in regard to the incidents. She came back home the next day from work and said, "She said she is proud of me," with all smiles. She was referring to her employer. I feel that those negative words over the years, really cut through to her core. I spoke *words of affirmation* a lot with her and I continue to do that because to me words of affirmation is a very significant language to her. Or better still, there is the possibility that she has a dual love language. I mean words of affirmation and receiving meaningful gifts as her primary love languages.

Remember that I said that she had gone into the 'I don't care mode', but then, with years of speaking the love languages, there is a different story. She actually cares! Sometimes, she threw in the "I don't care" phrase, but her actions showed otherwise. This was a step towards the right direction. It is wonderful. Although I am intentional with words of affirmation and I speak it fluently to my daughter, she still put pressure on herself to not make a mistake, she is still anxious. This is as a result of the parenting 'anyhow'. I am intentionally nurturing through my apprenticeship; it is only a matter of time that she would work through this for herself to remove the pressure she puts on herself. I am delighted to be a committed apprentice, progressing every day in my apprenticeship in the face of 'too late syndrome.'

I do the same with my son. I showed him how to make his bed in the mornings. He makes his bed, however not 'perfectly' but it is ok. It is a matter of timings when to give instructions for quality improvement. I commend him for taking his time to do it. I tell him that it was so helpful when I had to tidy up the bedrooms in the mornings. Since then, he does it every day and every day I praise him for it. I also tell him that one day he would teach his children how to make the bed and help his wife with tidying up around the home. I commend him for wiping the table. Sometimes he misses a spot and that is ok. I still commend him. When he is about to do it the next day though I might say something to point him in the right direction. I always make sure to appreciate his taking his time to do it and thank him for his effort. This way he feels valued and he feels that he is contributing to something and also learning something for his future family. He is always glad that he is helpful and whenever I say to him that he is helpful, you should see the smile on his face when he says, "really?" in a very satisfying and loving voice. Oh, it is priceless!

Now that he feels loved for his efforts and contributions, I take the opportunity to give him a few guidance to improve his bed making when I think it is necessary. It is all about timings. The times that I had come up with a few tips for improvements, he had taken them well because he also wants to enhance his bed making skills. I always speak his primary love language after that. His primary love language is not words of affirmation although he enjoys and receives affirmation very well. His primary love language is physical touch. If you remember from before, I have already highlighted all teenagers require their primary love language first and foremost as the foundation, however they require the other four as well. Just like I do!

Words of affection

Words of affection according to Dr Chapman is 'verbally expressing positive regard for the teenager as a person.' It does not focus on the teenagers' positive behaviour. Words of affection can focus on the body or personality of your teenager. Here are my phrases that I use with my daughter and my son. You are welcome to magpie and or make your own:

- **I adore you**
- **you are my world**
- **how did I become so blessed to have you?**
- **I love you for you**

- **You are beautiful/handsome**
- **You are so talented and gifted**
- **You sing beautifully**
- **You are so caring**
- **You are a blessing**
- **You look good**
- **I am blessed to be your mother**
- **I am humbly proud of you when I think of you**
- **My Sunflower**
- **I enjoyed our time together**
- **I admire you**
- **Your hair is amazing**
- **You are wise: Thank you for your advice/suggestion**
- **I appreciate you**
- **Thank you for sharing**
- **My Hope**

These are some of the words of affection that I have used and continue to use for my daughter and my son. Saying the three-word sentence: "I love you" is very important and crucial to our children and maturing adults. However, it is sad to say that a lot of teenagers do not hear their parents speaking these words to them for whatever reason. I must say that mothers and fathers speaking these words to one another in the presence of the children brings joy and love to the children.

I actually did use "I love you" to my children when I was parenting but not as much as I should have, although I loved my children. When I was growing up, no one spoke those words to me nor my siblings. And as a parent, I think I lacked the understanding of the impact that it may have on the teenager's life. Like me, there are many parents who also did not hear their parents say "I love you" to them. According to Dr Chapman, teenagers who did not hear these words from their parents may experience profound emotional pain. No matter what the reason is, I have learned that I could not let my children go through life without hearing "I love you" from me. I decided to rain them into their lives. And all the other phrases above; I shower them into their lives; I sprinkle them into their lives; I hail them into their lives; you name it.

My daughter and son are different people and I have learned to meet their needs through different routes. My son is the one-to-one, physical touch loved-up person. My daughter on the other hand will not give me the time of day. She was not available; she would prefer to be in her room or on her phone. So, I reached her through text messages. I spoke the words to my son and occasionally text him whereas I spoke and continue to speak the words to my daughter through text messages and occasionally speak the words to her face to face when I got the opportunity. As you are already aware, I started with my daughter when our situation was difficult so I made it a point to text her every day. I did this even though I did not receive any responses from her. It was difficult but I kept going, I kept texting her with various combinations of words of praise and words of affection. I was sincere with what I was doing, so I kept going.

There were times that she had even blocked me from her phone but I did not know so I kept texting. Even when I knew that she blocked me from time to time did not deter me. I continued and persevered. I did this for years, I still do. Sometimes I stick them on the cereal or put a note in the pack lunch. I sometimes wrote them notes and left them on their beds. I learned to show my gratitude and appreciation in all sorts of ways and mannerisms through words of affirmation and the other 4 languages. I will share some of the messages for my daughter and son in the chapter 18.

I would like to point out that I developed the skill to be quick to speak positively and encourage or show appreciation or recognition in a timely manner, rather than point out mistakes or omissions. Yes me, that is how far I have come – amazing! Anyway, why am I pointing this out? What I have realised is that negative attitude parents are quick to react to negatives than we recognise positives. Sometimes we feel that the positive is small and so insignificant. We are waiting for something huge, which means we would be waiting forever. We put huge expectations on our children who just want to be loved regardless of their mistakes. Many a time, as parents, giving or not giving our love become tied to whether they behave well or bad. That is conditional loving. We unknowingly want them to earn our love. As we continue to wait forever, our senses are heightened to seeing all the mistakes and omissions. We become frustrated over time and angry and then the negative words and the criticisms increase. This rings a bell to me because that was me before I became a committed apprentice.

What I have observed recently in a number of parents and whilst talking to others is that when their teenagers did some things that required recognition the parents didn't even acknowledge them, let alone respond to them. The times that they actually recognised and admitted that something was good, the parents delayed in their feedback. When I actually suggested that it would be a good thing to commend their teenagers immediately, they usually came out to say that "I will commend him or her later, I am busy right now". However, if the situation was one that called for rebuke, that action would have been carried out without delay. Why is that? I used to do that too. That is negative parenting, so watch out!

Words in the presence of others.

This is exactly as the name suggests. Affirm your teenager in the presence of others. It could be in the presence of siblings or wider family members. Beware though doing it in presence of his or her peers. You must tread carefully with that. Sometimes technology is good and we must use it to enhance our lives as and when appropriate. My daughter created a family group for her younger brother, herself and I sometime in 2020. We still use it now. When I do not have the opportunity to speak together as a group, I use the group chat on What's app. I have taken this opportunity to affirm them on this group chat. They are both aware of what I am commending and praising and what words of affection I am saying for them. It is amazing because almost every day I put my words of affirmation there for both of them although I speak to my son on one-to-one as well.

Then one Christmas, I wrote them each a letter and read them in the presence of the family on Boxing Day. Enjoy the details of the letters in chapter 18. I tell you as soon as I finished reading the letters, my daughter and my son, both came to me and hugged me with tears in their eyes. Everyone present was touched. It felt good. It was such an amazing experience even for me. I had not done something like this on a bigger scale so I was thrilled. According to Dr Chapman this may speak more deeply to my daughter's and son's need for emotional love than if I had just done it with just the three of us. It has an even bigger impact when done in the presence of others. For my teenagers and I the impact was bigger and everyone present was touched with love, I would say!

Be mindful of the tongue. Be intentional about the words that proceeds from your mouth because:

'Death and life are in the power of the tongue, and those who love it will eat its fruit.' – Proverbs 18:21

Chapter 13

Lesson 10: Loving through touch

Loving through touch is what Dr Chapman calls, *Physical touch.* It is powerful, no wonder mothers are encouraged to touch their babies soon after birth for love and bonding. A baby that was not touched would eventually fail to thrive. We are such social beings that thrive on physical touch. For some people physical touch communicate more to them than any other love language. I would say that my son is one of such people. From cuddling to tickling, you name it. Teenagers are a little complicated and as parents we must learn how to communicate physical touch. Because they are growing in independence and finding themselves, communicating love through physical touch may depend on a few things such as when, where and how.

Timings

This is so important because when you get the timing wrong as a parent your good intentions would backfire. Dr Chapman explains that speaking this language is difficult because it is largely determined by the mood of the teenager and we all know that a teenager's mood is never consistent. This is so true. I have been doing it for years and I still get it wrong sometimes with my daughter even now. This is largely due to the fact that my daughter's mood is never consistent. I have therefore learned to let her take the initiative most of the time; however occasionally when I suspect that she would welcome that, then I would go for it. Thank God, her primary love language is not physical touch. She has her own moments when she would take the initiative and cuddle up with me in bed. She may sometimes ask me to plait her hair although this rarely happens these days. Most definitely, when she was crying, she would welcome physical touch through a hug or a cuddle or a pat on her back. With my daughter though when she has had enough, she would indicate for me to leave her alone by shrugging her shoulders or wriggle out of my embrace. Sometimes it would be a long cuddle during which I may even sing for her and or pray in my heart. Other times for a short time, just long enough for me to say the words, 'everything will be OK, or 'I love you.' I have learned and come to understand these dynamics from her.

My son on the other hand is all physical touch loved-up. From cuddles, to hugs, to tickles, to kisses, to touching my hands and his hand. Holding hands and cuddling up in the sofa is amazing. Any form of body touch, count my son in. From leaning on me to stroking. We have even come out with our own term: 'strokey strokey' is the favourite one. He strokes my cheeks with his cheeks. Yes, I know! He is 13 years now and I am waiting to see whether he would require me to speak a different dialect of the language as he gets older. I am waiting for it. At the moment, whereas I used to give him a hug as soon as I collected him from school when he was in primary school, I do not do that much now that he is in secondary school. I may give him a high five or cuddle in the car. He always welcomes it. We have even developed our own unique way of saying Bye when I drop him off to school through a form of physical touch.

I guess I am also learning with him. Whereas I started at a difficult stage with my daughter, I am learning from the beginning with my son. My son will not shrug or resist a physical touch from me. Even when he says, "Leave me alone" when he is upset; he would always crumble and succumb with physical touch. You see what I mean when I say different nurturing needs with my daughter and son. When you ask my son, 'How do you feel Mummy's love?' he would say, "Mummy loves me because she cuddles me, gives me lots of hugs and takes care of me."

Nuggets for your bag.

- Let me share something that I discovered learning the art of speaking love languages. I remember when I was doing 'anyhow' parenting, I had learned that when you discipline your child for bad behaviour and you give them a hug after the discipline, it created confusion and inconsistency for the child. Here I was now, I had to unlearn that to relearn that actually it is a good thing to speak the child's or teenager's primary love language shortly after discipline. According to Dr Chapman, the discipline is for the bad behaviour and the hug is for him or her as a person. In other words, expressing love to our teenagers should be expressed regardless of whatever the behaviour. I am pleased to inform you that it works magic. I discipline my teenagers and speak their love languages to them shortly after that and it has been absolutely great. My daughter and my son have both responded very well to this.

- My son loves his soft toys and blankets. He enjoys the soft touch and that is reassuring for him. He finds comfort from the touch. I usually would buy him a soft teddy and he loves it. We would enjoy a pillow fight together. I would suggest presents or gifts which are soft to touch for teenagers whose love language is physical touch.

- Hugs and kiss my son every day.

- We have our own handshake and greeting.

- I tuck him in bed most nights and kiss him good night. The nights that he would already be in bed, I would stroke his cheeks and give him a kiss and cover him up. If he was not already fast asleep, he sometimes mumbled "I love you Mama". So, rewarding!

- My son asked me the other day, "Mummy..." and I responded, "Yes, LD". He continued, "Why did God invent hugs? It's so lovely and I feel so happy when you hug me and I know that everything will be okay." My response was, "That is exactly why God created hugs, He wants you to feel exactly the way you do. I love you."

I will end this lesson by sharing that:

'Let us love one another, for love is of God; and everyone who loves is born of God and knows God ... God is love.' – I John 4:7 and 8

Chapter 14

Lesson 11: Loving through Gifts

There are people that the love language that speaks most to them is gifts. The language of gift is simply giving and receiving meaningful gifts. A gift becomes meaningful especially when it has a story attached to it such as history or when it carries an encouragement or inspiration for the future. I remember when my daughter first completed a questionnaire for her love language. From that questionnaire, the love language of gifts is her primary love language. I have mentioned that I have used words of affirmation a lot with my daughter because of our circumstance. I have also mentioned that she has been experiencing panic attacks, anxiety and has lost her confidence. I have used gifts as well and I continue to use it. At the time when I identified her love language as gifts through the questionnaire, I was not quite sure that it was right. However, I learned to speak the language to her regardless. More recently, I have realised that she has been speaking the language of gifts a lot to others. In fact, I have been a beneficiary of this. Her brother is also benefiting from her speaking of this language as well as her friends and other members of the family. According to Dr Chapman, we tend to speak our own primary love language to others because it comes naturally to us thinking that others receive love in the same primary love language as we do.

Let me share an interesting observation with you. Prior to realising that my daughter's love language is gifts, I was giving her gifts but not meaningful gifts. What I realised though was that, she bought gifts for herself and friends. She never bought me or her brother or her father gifts then. What was intriguing was that, anytime she bought a present for someone, she would end up taking part of the present for herself. She admitted this and used to talk about it. I did not understand what that meant or why she did that. I probably thought at the time that she was being selfish. Fast forward, after years of being a committed apprentice, speaking her primary love language and all the others, now she actually gives gifts without tampering with them. I have observed her several times buying gifts for people including myself, my son, her aunties, and cousins and her friends. She cares and takes time to shop online of course (it's lockdown) for the presents although she finds it tricky wrapping them. I sometimes wrap them for her. I will share with you my first gift I received from her.

She had been working her part time job from around mid-June 2017, she was 16 years old. She had her pay regularly each month. That was when she used to buy things for herself. She bought clothes and make-up among other things. I had become a committed apprentice around the end of 2016 and learning by the day. It was 2018 December Christmas time that my son and I received Christmas presents from my daughter. Mind you, she had been working for almost a year and a half receiving monthly payments. It had taken me two years of being a committed apprentice, intentionally loving my daughter before she started speaking love to me in her primary love language. I was surprised what I received from her: she bought me two presents for that Christmas. She bought me a wrist watch and the Google version of Alexa. We had gone to Westfield Shopping Centre (we visited Westfield often in those times) just spending time together through in the shops. We were talking about something and I had mentioned that I would prefer to tell time from a watch rather than having to check the time from my phone. As we were talking, I talked about "OK Google" that is Google's smart speaker. And to my amazement come Christmas day, those very things that I talked about were the very same presents she got for me. I had no idea she was going to do that. She had never bought me presents so I was not expecting anything from her. What really touched me was the fact that she actually was listening to me when I was talking with her that day at Westfield. To me, that alone meant a lot and spoke a lot to me. I felt loved. The gifts actually did cost her quite a lot of money, but she gave freely. The presents brought tears to my eyes when I opened them. I knew I had my daughter back.

It was still a long road ahead but I knew that we were on the same right road together.

Most recently, I received a text from her telling me that she was ordering a really nice pretty notebook for herself as she wanted to start journaling. She thought that I would like one so she sent me the link to choose one. In fact, she had selected one that she thought I would like and sent it to me via What's app. She ordered the books and when the books arrived, she exchanged hers with me when I expressed interest in the design of the book she chose for herself. Even when I said she could have her original book, she insisted that it was okay for me to keep it. She is speaking the love language of gifts more and more and this is making me realise that the result of the initial questionnaire was right. To me, it appears that she may have a dual primary love language. Not only is she speaking gifts she is also beginning to speak words of affirmation. I started this journey when my daughter was in the 'too late syndrome' and 'I don't care mode', it has taken quite sometime of intentional nurturing to arrive where we are now.

This was the conversation that transpired between my daughter and I in regards to the pretty notebook:

Daughter: "Hey Mum, I'm gonna order a pretty notebook for myself. There's lots of pretty ones so you can pick which one u like?" Then she sends me a link. "Would you like this one?"

Me: "Yes. Thanks. Very thoughtful. What did I do?"

Daughter: "What? Nothing lol I wanted a notebook to start keeping a diary for myself and I saw some really pretty ones that I think you'd like. ☺"

Me: "Aww thanks, I think it's an amazing idea keeping journal/diary."

Daughter: "Thank you. ☺"

This was such a fulfilling moment because it has taken us a while getting here. This was so beautiful and rewarding and good because of the process that we had gone through to get here. I am grateful that I did, it is worth every pain, every challenge and every difficulty I have gone through to arrive here. The feeling is just precious.

As if this was not enough, as I sat down editing this piece of writing on one beautiful day, a delivery came through. We were still in lockdown, waiting to hear from Boris with an update regarding easing measures for March, 2021. She went to the door to receive the parcel. She brought it to the kitchen and unpacked it. I was busy writing until I heard her voice, "Mum this is for you". To my amazement she was holding a mug with the inscription "I'M A GREAT MUM, THIS MUG SAYS SO." My heart just melted. She said that is what she thinks of me. I realised that indeed gifts mean a lot to my daughter. What was more, she is feeling loved enough to actually also speak love to me. And for her to express that she thinks I am a great mum is the strawberries, blueberries, bananas and honey on my pancakes. Just Delish! This is the same child who used to tell me that she hates me, the same child that used to tell me that I stress her out, this was the same child who used to blocked me from her phone. This was the same 'alien' that was on my door step. The 'alien' has indeed vomited my baby girl out from its belly.

In fact, when my daughter was younger, she had lots of gifts from her father and I. Her father especially would buy her gadgets, I mean the latest tech, for doing something good or achieving something. This was usually achievement of good work at school. According to Dr Chapman, this is not speaking the primary love language of gift. This was payment for something that she earned. Speaking the love through gifts is different. According to Dr Chapman, a gift is something that the teenager does not deserve or did not earn. It is given purely out of unconditional love from the parent to the teenager. Do you know something, the day I came to this knowledge, I realised that all these years that we were giving 'gifts' to our daughter, we thought we were loving her? However, I know now that we were actually paying her for services rendered. I even remember that sometimes when we bought her an expensive birthday present because we thought she earned it for doing or achieving something. We would actually tell her that she earned it so that she would continue to work hard to earn the 'gifts.'

The day I came to this understanding I realised that we have not loved our daughter at all in a way and manner for her to receive love. We had loved her conditionally. Most of the 'gifts' we gave her if not all were simply payments for services or achievements. How awful to swallow this? You see what ignorance does? It makes you behave foolishly. It makes you wise in your own eyes but in truth you are foolish. That is the bottom line. I am not saying that giving your teenagers presents for doing something or achieving something is wrong, what I have learnt is that it is not speaking the love language gifts as it is not a gift according to Dr Chapman. I immediately realised how foolish I had been. My daughter's emotional love tank must have been dried empty; I mean empty to the core. No wonder, although my daughter wanted to speak the love language of gifts to her friends, she ended up tampering with the gifts.

The teenager years are challenging for both parents and teenagers. Many parents find themselves cutting deals with their teenagers through manipulation to get teenagers to do what we as parents would like them to do. This is where the conditional sentences come in. "If you do ... then I would do..." For example, "If you sweep the kitchen, I will get you ice cream." In essence you want to get some work out of your teenager before you give him or her the ice cream. Now although you might think that you are doing your teenager a favour or loving them by getting them ice cream, according to Dr Chapman, the ice cream is not a gift. It is a payment for sweeping the kitchen. Your teenager would take the ice cream as something he or she deserved because she/he worked for it. It was not a gift. Like my daughter's father and I, we thought we were expressing love to our daughter but our daughter received those items as things that she had worked for; she deserved them.

I am not saying that don't cut deals with your teenagers, what I am saying here is that don't be confused or get it twisted that you are loving your teenager through gifts. In fact, teenagers also enjoy cutting deals with their parents these days because they have realised that this has become the way they would get what they want. It is happening in many homes. To me this is manipulation in a way. I have become very conscious and intentional whenever I am using a sentence that has the "If...then...". I really think about it in terms of its implications. I have trained myself to remove that phrase from my vocabulary as much as possible.

Speaking this language initially with my daughter was a challenge because, she was in the too late syndrome, 'I don't care mode' and I was closed to her world to some extent. Giving gifts as love has to be meaningful in order to speak to my daughter. One of the first gifts I gave to my daughter that I would say spoke to her was a small decorative mother and daughter sculpture I picked form a local shop. The reason why I knew that it spoke love to her was the fact that one day, the head of the mother broke off as it dropped off from her table. My daughter was disappointed. I tried so many ways to fix it, until one day I managed to fix it. You should see the delight in her eyes and the smiles on her face when she found the head attached. It was brilliant. I also bought her a small pot of yellow artificial followers. I had realised that she was down for a couple of days and I wanted to do something to cheer her up. I bought her this pot of flowers and a card with the notes "I hope this brings a smile to your face." I can tell you that she still has this on her table in her room. My daughter likes money so sometimes I may put £5 or £10 note for her to buy something nice for herself.

I did similar things for her brother. My son needs are different from my daughter and whereas gifts are my daughter's primary language, it is not for my son. I spoke this language to my son too. For him I usually got him soft gifts with touch essence because his primary love language is physical touch. I would usually get him a soft teddy or a jumper or T shirt that is soft to the skin.

When I get them gifts, I take my time to wrap them. I may present them in presence of family or just place it on their bed. You know what? If for instance their beds were not made for that day, I would go further to speak the language of acts of service and make their beds and then place the gift on the bed. I can tell you that I really enjoyed loving and serving my teenagers in this manner.

When do I speak this love language?

- What I tend to do is that when I discipline them or bring something that I think requires improvement, I may speak this love language shortly after the this.

- Sometimes I just tell them how grateful I am to be their mother and how blessed I am to have them as my children. I may speak this love language to them.

- I speak this love language at Birthdays and at Christmas

- I may speak this love language to my daughter when she is down

- Sometimes when we are celebrating anything. And I must tell you I have intentionally made a point to celebrate the smallest of things. We celebrate at the end of the month for loving ourselves and loving others throughout the month.

- No particular occasion. Just for the reason of loving my teenagers.

I would like to put forward that the love language of gifts has nothing to do with the cost of the gift. Gifts for your teenagers do not have to be necessarily costly. If that were the case I would have been priced out. I concentrate on the simple things that interest my teenagers. What is important is the time and the effort I take to make it happen. Things like the wrapping paper, or the ceremony or the story that comes with it. I shared in an earlier chapter about giving words of affirmation to my teenagers in the presence of our family. I chose the occasion of a Boxing Day when the family was all together relaxing. I also gave my daughter a gift and my son a gift after the words of affirmation from the letter. I beautifully wrapped Oreo biscuits because they both enjoy Oreo biscuits.

What an amazing way of unconditionally loving my teenagers and also modelling for them to love through giving freely.

'Freely you have received, freely give.' – *Matthew 10:8*

Chapter 15

Lesson 12: Loving through spending time together

L oving through spending *quality time* can be quite challenging because one thing that parents struggle with is time. The world is so much in a hurry that we barely have any time for anything. We are rushed and busy. We are so focused on our jobs that we end up saying to our teenagers, "I don't have time" or "Can't you see I'm busy?" For years I gave the spare of me, the spare time of me and the spare energy of me to my children. I resolved to change that when I became a committed apprentice. I have come to the conclusion that as parents we cannot say we want the best for our children and teenagers and not make time for them. I intentionally spend time with my teenagers together. I have two of them as you may be aware by now. It is important to highlight that sometimes we may be in the same house with our teenagers and even in the same room however this does not mean we are together with our teenagers. There were times when my daughter was in such a state that although she was in the house, I felt that she was far away. It feels like being there by not there; there was no connection.

For me quality time is spending time with my teenagers doing what they want to do. I also spend time with them doing what we all want to do sometimes. I give them my time to show interest in them. I am intentional about this. I must say that I find speaking this language with my son quite easy compared to my daughter. My son is available whilst my daughter is not. My daughter and I do get some moments to have quality time though. Again, different needs are resurfacing here. As already pointed out my daughter is nearly 7 years older than her younger brother. I missed out on spending time with my daughter when she was my son's age because I was not intentional and because I was doing 'anyhow' parenting at the time. And now that I want to spend quality time with her, she is not available. I will encourage you:

- Please do not waste the time you have now to be intentional and take your apprenticeship seriously. Spend quality time with your teenagers.

- The younger the better because they are more bendable, flexible and cooperative and they have the time to be around you. They are more engaging.

- The older they get the more difficult it becomes if you have not already laid the pipework. I mean the foundation.

- The older they get, they are less flexible, they have less time, they're hanging out with their friends, they are in their own world doing their own stuff. It is important that teenagers spend time with their friends. It is part of their independence and as parents we must not take it personally.

- They also become moody the older they get.

I spend a lot of quality time with my son: we talk about life. Anything about life from sex to his games and everything in between. We talk about drugs. We talk about smoking, money, credit cards, boyfriends/ girlfriends, sperms, periods, you name it. we talk about his games, his favourite ones (Pokémon and Minecraft) and his television programmes (SpongeBob). We laugh and joke around. You should see him when he talks about his games and television programmes. He is so excited about them, and I become excited about them because he is so excited about them. We laugh about the silly things that the characters in the TV programmes do and we actually laugh a lot. It is so fulfilling. He would end up saying 'I love you Mummy.' My heart would just melt as I responded with a hug and "I love you too, LD". I call him LD sometimes.

The most important thing is we have fun doing it. We talk about sadness, joy, peace, faith and fear. When I am sad, he gives me a cuddle and when he is sad, I give him a cuddle and we do this whilst spending time together. We talk about different types of friendships and the development of friendships. For example, now he differentiates his friendships. He tells me, this person is his "acquaintance, casual friend or close friend." Before we discussed friendships, he used to use a blanket word: friend. From this angle he is beginning to learn the basis for establishing intimate relationships. I believe that this will be very important and useful when he starts dating in the future.

Let me share with you something we do every night. The hour before his bedtime is one of the allocated times (secured times) when we have our quality time. During this time, we turn all screens off. We talk about the day; we take turns to share about how we have loved ourselves and others. We share with each other how we have been considerate and sacrificed appropriately. We will read a chapter that he chooses from the bible; I will tickle his feet or underarms and he would tickle my feet sometimes; or we have pillow fights depending on what he wanted to do. We would say our prayers then I would tuck him in bed, sing a song we both love:

"Jesus loves me this I know, For the bible tells me so, little ones to Him belong. They are weak but he is strong. Yes, Jesus loves me; Yes, Jesus loves you; Yes, Jesus loves us; For the bible tells me son."

And then I kiss him good night. This has become a routine for us that we both enjoy. I intend to be intentional about doing this for as long as my son would allow me to do as he grows older. I will keep you posted in the future. I must confess that this has strengthened the bond that my son and I share. I admit that I did not have the same level of attention and time for my daughter when she was my son's age. I missed out big time and now that I would like to have some quality time with her, she is not available. Most of the time she is doing her own things or with her friends. The important thing is that she is however aware that I am always available to her.

I decided that instead of waiting for her to come to me I would share my life with her. How was I going to do this? I came to the decision that I would write her a letter each month sharing my life with her, rather than waiting for her to share her life with me. In that way I would be spending time with her indirectly. In preparation, I went out one day and bought a small fit-for-purpose gift box, big enough for her to store the letters I would send her. The plan was that each month I would drop a letter on her bed. I thought to myself that, she did not have to read them straight away and even when she did read them, she would have a place to store them safely. I also would intentionally add a small gift each time I drop the letter. I know she likes banana bread. A piece of banana bread beautifully wrapped would speak so much to her. I am hoping that this would speak to her emotionally and also keep her in anticipation for the next drop. I can't wait! I am intentionally thinking about ways to be a nurturing mother and the Holy Spirit supports me with this.

Recently, I thought that it would be nice to have some quality time together as a family. We all discussed it and agreed that one day a week would be set aside when we would have dinner together as a family and spend time together after dinner either share a movie or play games or cards. My son and I enjoy this family night each week except the times when he went to his fathers for the weekend. My daughter on the other hand, did not participate as much as my son and I would have liked. Sometimes she was out with her friends, other times she would prefer to be in her room. Thank God quality time is not the primary love language for my daughter. There is always teething problems when you initially start anything new. So, I am patient and consistent with it. I know that over time things would improve. I am not giving up; the night is set and for me it is a family tradition.

I am not suggesting that parents reading my story have to do the same things I am doing or I have done with my teenagers. What I am hoping is that you would find your own way of speaking these languages by using my ways as the basis for ideas. By all means try mine if it works for you however your teenagers might respond to different things. I would suggest though that first take your parenting apprenticeship seriously and be a committed apprentice and all these things will fall into place. Believe me they will begin to make sense just as they did for me. You are not on your own on the journey of parenting

116

apprenticeship. I brought my burden and laid it down at His feet. You can do the same but it is entirely your call. As I have already pointed out, I am learning from the best. It works!

> *'Come to Me all you who labour and are heavy laden, and I will give you rest…learn from me, for I am lowly in heart and you will find rest for your souls.' – Matthew 11:28-29*

Chapter 16

Lesson 13: Loving through serving

L oving through service is simply means doing things for your loved ones. In my situation and for the purposes of this book, it means serving our children and teenagers. It ranges from fixing them food to supporting them with their homework. From doing laundry for them to making their beds. It also includes the things or the life skills that we teach them when they are teenagers. So that from doing everything for them when they were younger, we move to teaching them to doing things for themselves in order to also encourage their sense of independence and development. It is very important to do it in a loving and nurturing manner so that it will carry with it the emotional love that it is meant to communicate to your teenager.

Before I became a committed apprentice, I did acts of service for my daughter, however I also felt that she must be appreciative of what I was doing for her. My expectation therefore began to consume me so that all I looked out for was this gratitude from my daughter, which at the time was also not forth coming. So, I was upset and critical of the fact that she was ungrateful. What was more, I also compared what I did for her, to what I received at her age from my parents and that even increased my demand for appreciation. What happened was the more I demanded, the more she resisted to show any appreciation. In fact, I think that because I was so frustrated at her lack of gratitude, I became quite critical of the acts of services she carried out at home and picked on the things that she did not do well. In the end, the things that I had taught her to do around the home such as cleaning the bath room, she even stopped doing it because I guess that not only did I not show appreciation for her efforts, she felt that she could not please me because I was just critical.

I wanted so much appreciation that I was blinded and did not show any appreciation towards her for the things she did around the home. I mean how could I demand appreciation from her when I did not appreciate her or what she did? I am sharing this because as parents we want our teenagers to behave in a certain way but then we behave in another. How was she going to learn to be appreciative when I did not show her meaningful appreciation for what she did? Of course, when she was little, I thought her to be grateful and say her 'thank yous' for things done for her and for presents given to her. She did that as a young child with no questions, however now that she is a teenager or a maturing adult, it is part of the process and the development for her to be analytical and reason on a different level because of her need for independence and development of self-worth and identity. This meant that she questioned things and would not accept things at face value like she did when she was younger. And as a parent it was my responsibility to be a loving leader to her. I learned this when I became a committed apprentice. That is, I lead by example, I actually model things for her, that means if I wanted appreciation from her, I knew I must show appreciation for things that she did and appreciate her as a person too. I wanted her to respect me so I must respect her. Teenagers lose trust and respect for their parents because sometimes parents expect their teenagers to act in one way, however they (parents) act in a different way. That is double standards and whilst your teenagers did not question you (parent) on this when they were younger, they would now that they are teenagers. Some teenagers might actually say this to their parents especially in heated arguments, or they might just keep it to themselves.

I learned knew ways to communicate this language to my teenagers at an emotional level to fill their love tank. I changed my attitude of wanting and demanding appreciation from my daughter and my son to not expecting anything in return in the manner I shared in an earlier chapter in this book. I learned to busy myself to serve my children in a way that would speak love to them. I would cook, clean and tidy up after them most of the time. The days that my teenagers would clean up after themselves, I would show appreciation and be grateful for their help. My daughter was able to clean after herself and take care of her environment. She made the decision when to. She was also able to cook simple meals although she seldomly did at home. The good thing was I have had good feedback from people that my daughter is amazing at taking care of 'business'. Once, I had to go away for a few days so I asked my older sister to come and stay with them at home. And the feedback I had from sister was, "Your daughter is brilliant, she did everything." The problem is my daughter says "I can't be bothered to do stuff at home sometimes." By that she meant when I was around.

Being human sometimes I felt that it would be good if my teenagers actually did more around the house to help. Whenever I felt this way, my mood went into "Who cares about me?" and "My teenagers do not care about me." I continued to work through it hoping to see some changes in their behaviour. I realised that having this expectation (to see change in behaviour) although it was subconscious effected my behaviour. There would be occasions when I will find myself sad, uncared for and unloved. This was something that was happening on and off and eventually I was able to manage it. I had learned how to speak my feelings and concerns to my teenagers without attacking them with my words. But because my teenagers were used to me attacking or accusing them or being critical in the past, they had to learn to recognise the change in my communication and then learn to decide to respond in an appropriate manner. This was particularly challenging with my daughter. This took time and patience, because it is a process and a journey.

Most of the time I had kept my consistency, whilst other times I had not done as well as I would have hoped. For example, when the thoughts of 'Who is caring for me, who is loving me, or when I feared that my teenagers may be irresponsible or I was thinking, "what will people think' resurface, that was when I may up the volume on my voice. So, this was an intentional nurturing management programme. When this happened, I went back to explain and apologise for my behaviour not my concerns but for the way I behaved or handled it. This has been going well because, the stress and frustrations levels are low and has made the environment such a nurturing one. My son usually says, "Mum, I love our home, it's happy here". I would just look at him with a smile on my face and say, "I love it here too and I am glad you do too". That is a nurturing home environment.

It is amazing having a Supervisor on this journey. I contacted my Supervisor for help with my fears. Since I have become intentional and a committed apprentice, my hearing to the voice of God has enhanced. I reflect constantly and meditate so that I hear God speaking to me through people and things around me without even speaking to them. Sometimes from watching a movie or a tv programme the very thing I was questioning; I get an answer to it. It is amazing and a miracle; God is all around us. God is indeed with us. I have the experience of it and I am sharing it with you. One day as I was reflecting with my Supervisor, I walked into my bedroom. My radio was tuned into a Christian radio station and as I walked in, it appeared that there was a teaching session going on and the speaker was a female. Suddenly, I heard her explain that as parents we do the cooking and then end up doing the dishes after everyone else. And we feel tired and sad and upset thinking, "Who cares about me?" What she went on to say was that "Do everything as onto the Lord. You are doing it for the Lord. He cares and loves you. Do not look at your children or young people or whoever you are doing it for, do it as onto the Lord." That was it for me. There and then I got the answer I was looking for. How joyful and peaceful to receive direction and guide to things that concern me as a mother and a parent. I want you to experience it for yourself, it is wonderful! Be a committed apprentice and be at peace.

Just the other day, my daughter put her clothes in the wash. When the clothes were done, there were things on the line so she couldn't dry them straight after. Eventually when I removed the things from the line, I decided to put her things on the line for her (acts of service). A day after I had put her things on the line, she came to the washing machine to attempt to dry her things. She opened the machine only to find it empty and then she looked on the line and there, her things staring at her. Then she looked at me "My clothes..." and I said, "Yes, your clothes, I put them on the line yesterday." She said, "Oh, thank you, I did not realise." Now this is an example of act of service. I have loved through my service and I could tell from the way she expressed her appreciation that she was actually touched and felt loved. Sometimes I go the extra mile of doing her wash, drying it out and folding it for her. I sometimes do this when she is not home. This is an act of service, which I sprinkle from time to time to communicate love to my teenagers.

My son is 13 years old and I have taught him to make his bed and wash his plates and clean up the dining table after dinner. One day, I said to him, "LD, I love you very much. When you were little, I did everything for you, now that you are a maturing adult, I would like to teach you to do certain things for yourself so that you would be able to do it for yourself when you are at university; you will be able to help your future wife and also teach your own children. Because I love you so much and I do not want to do you a disservice by doing it for you all the time like I used to, it is important that I teach you." I explained to him that I could continue to do everything for him, however that would not be loving him, I would be doing him a disservice. He understood that and welcomed my service of teaching him to be independent. He now makes his bed, cleans the table, washes his plates, does the laundry and takes the recycling bin out on bin collection days. I show him the most appreciation for his efforts all the time. I must say that I am intentional to go all out with my appreciation. I do not focus on the fact that it is done well or not. I reward efforts and he progress and grows in these areas. Sometimes I might wash his plate or make his bed for him when he is running late or we might do the laundry together to encourage him. This is loving him through service, we enjoy doing it together without the pressure and this way love is in the air. One thing I have learned from the language of *acts of service* is the fact that when I teach my son how to do something, it does not mean that I never have to do it again for him or I have to expect that he would do it all the time and to the standard that I expect. No! I have learned to be flexible and adaptable knowing that I am doing this as onto the Lord.

So, whenever I have to teach him something new, I explain the love I have for him by using the 'disservice illustration' and then I follow it up with his primary love language which is physical touch (hug or rub on his shoulders or arm). He usually welcomes it without hesitation. My next thing to teach him is ironing his school uniforms. I am only teaching him, however from time to time I would do it for him or we would do the ironing together.

Intentionally loving my teenagers means a lot to me. Not only have I grown in the process, but it is growing the relationship between my teenagers and I in a fruitful manner. I still speak the love languages whether my teenagers behave themselves or not. Speaking the love languages is my unconditional love for my children. I love them because they are my children and they do not have to do anything to be loved by me. I have learned unconditional love which has been made possible because I became a committed apprentice. I have been enabled to establish a nurturing home environment for my teenagers from where they can have the emotional stability to navigate and grow the physical, social, emotional, psychological and spiritual spheres of their lives. Nurturing my teenagers is so enjoyable, because there is less frustration, anger and arguments. There is so much joy and peace in my home now. I would share some messages in the last module to give you insight and understanding of the fruits of being a committed apprentice. For now, I would encourage you to serve your teenagers as doing it on to the Lord.

'And whatever you do, do it heartily as to the Lord not to men, knowing that from the Lord you will receive reward.' –
Colossians 3:23

Reflections

Our perceptions and expectations have an impact on the way we receive and interpret messages. I have discovered that the messages that we receive from our children and teenagers can be seen as gold nuggets or bombshells. On reflection, I have come to the conclusion that I used to see and receive loads of messages as bombshells because of the premise I viewed them from. As a committed apprentice, I was taught another way that enabled me to comprehend the messages in even the most difficult and challenging of information as gold nuggets. I chose and still choose to stick with this new way which over the years has brought me much delight and joy. I am sharing this module package with you so that you may also see the light should you choose to see from this new way.

Some time ago, mothers from my support group called *Love* asked me to share with them the kind of messages that I send to my teenagers. So, I want to include in this module messages to support other mothers and parents who might be wondering where to start or how to go about it. I share messages with you that reflect on ways that I have come to condition the soil (environment) for nurturing my teenagers. I have become intentional in my purpose as a mother to water my seeds (teenagers) and prune (boundaries with love and sensitivity) my teenagers. Relax, enjoy and be intentionally informed.

Chapter 17

Gold Nuggets or Bombshells

I am sharing this chapter with you to actually capture the essence of what I mean when I talk about viewing an experience as a bombshell or as a gold nugget. I am going to share a text message conversation that took place between my daughter and I sometime in December, 2015. My daughter was 14 years 7months old then. I had not yet become a committed apprentice at the time. It was just the other day I was going over my text messages to my daughter and I came across this. I was shocked and saddened by the experience and I thought it would be worthwhile sharing with you. My daughter pours her heart out to me and my reaction? Well ... find out for yourself.

Daughter: "Mum I'm stuck. Do you ever have that feeling where you feel you are just stuck in life? As in you don't have much to look forward to and everything you want to do and achieve in life itself has been forgotten and all you can think about is being stuck. Stuck in a cycle of wake up, school, home, sleep again and again. The weekend only lasts so long before its back to that and then you remember that is what you are basically going to do for the rest of it. Nothing else. You are just stuck in a place where there is no way out than death itself. What else is there to do but live. That's what we are doing now and every day I am just describing my days more 'liveable' than anything else because that's what it all is. Liveable. If this is something I can look forward to then let it be."

Me: "I keep giving you chance after chance and you throw it back in my face."

Daughter: "Can't you see that I try harder and harder."

Me: "I know you trying…"

Daughter: "I don't even live anymore, I'm not even existing. I'm literally surviving here, in this world."

Me: "You need to try harder, surviving where?"

Daughter: "At least I am trying instead of putting in no efforts at all, in the world."

Me: "That is not the point. You know what to do. In life there are boundaries, responsibilities and fulfilment and you have to find the balance in order to be fulfilled. I am trying to show you because I love you and that is my job but you make it harder and harder for yourself and for me so then you lose your privileges as a result."

Daughter: "But that's not fair, I'm still growing up and I'm making mistakes. It's like you are punishing me for mistakes that everyone makes."

Me: "No my daughter. I appreciate your mistakes and expect you to recognise them and learn from them but you don't."

Daughter: "I TRY. How come I don't get any recognition from that"

Me: "Even when you are corrected, you don't appreciate that so you keep making the same mistakes over and over again."

Daughter: "You can't just keep me cooped up in here. Maybe if you let me do things that I want maybe there'll be a difference."

Me: "I am not judging you or making you feel bad…you have to make better choices. It does not work like that."

Daughter: "No you are judging me, everyone judges me and I hate it. I can't deal with this anymore. I don't want help; I HATE having help."

Me: "You have to sacrifice to get something. Until you accept that…"

Daughter: "I don't want to feel helpless when there are people *who need the help. I want to be on my own. It's not fair, none of it is, why won't you let me do anything?"*

Me: "You still don't understand"

Daughter: "You don't understand anything about me and the worst thing is that you don't want to."

Reading the conversations really saddens my heart. She was right, clearly, I did not understand. I did not have a clue what was going on. I just had a tunnel vision: my daughter was making mistakes and I wanted to make her correct those mistakes. That was it, I had no sense of the bigger picture. I have been able to come to this conclusion because I am now a committed apprentice and I have learned so much and gained understanding and wisdom, since the later part of 2016 when I decided to nurture my teenagers in a different way. The conversation clearly highlights that I was in my mode of 'corrections' and being critical to the extent that I did not give consideration to her feelings or thoughts. It was like I had to win and I had to show that I was the parent, the adult and it was my job. It was like I had to fix her behaviour or make her to change her behaviour.

The result was that the punishments became harsher and harsher, in my attempt to force her into submission, to force her to be the child that she was and admit that she was wrong and to change. But guess what, she was not a child any longer; she was a maturing adult, a teenager who was also looking for independence and developing a sense of her identity and self-worth. What I did not realise at the time was that she would make so many mistakes and regardless of those mistakes she was looking to be loved and accepted by her parents. What was sad was the fact that she was looking for words of affirmation for her efforts and comfort but she got none from me. It was almost like I was blinded to her efforts of trying and so I did not recognise them. My eyes could only see the things she was doing wrong. She felt that people were judging her from outside and she was being judged in her own home as well, by her own mother. I was so wrong. I did not have any insight and understanding into what was going on. I was doing what I thought had to be done, the way I knew how. I was far from the mark. I behaved in ignorance. As I have already pointed out behaving ignorantly with the best of intentions does not mean that you escape the consequences. And why was I ignorant? I was ignorant because I had not taken my apprenticeship seriously. I had taken things into my own hands. I was doing a job that required supervision without supervision. I was leaning on my own understanding. I was doing what was right in my own eyes and I was so off the mark.

I am not excusing the fact that my daughter made mistakes and continued to make those mistakes. Reading the messages now, I could see the frustration from her and I could also see the frustration from me too. We were both frustrated because we were both on different tangents. She was on Mars and I was on Jupiter. I did not empathise with her feelings at all, especially in her first text. That first message carried a lot of information that I could have unpicked if I were intentional enough but I missed it all. There is so much information there that tells me about her state of mind, the view of herself as a person and of life and the struggles she was going through. I can now even deduce from this message that she did not even see any kind of excitement and purpose from the lives of her parents. My daughter could see that our lives were not purposeful and not meaningful and thought, was that what the world was about? Was that what life was about? She could not see anything worthy to aspire to when she looked at the lives that her parents lived. She felt like she was drowning but I could not see that.

My approach to handling the whole conversation as a mother was wrong and made things worse for my daughter and for myself. The way and manner and the attitude with which I handled the situation is without a doubt that I received the message as a bombshell. I say it was a bombshell because that was how I reacted to the situation. I took the situation negatively and consequently dealt with it with a negative attitude. I did not recognise any positives or anything worthy of exploration and so my behaviour towards the experience was one of a negative approach. At the end my daughter left the conversation feeling depleted, unappreciated, misunderstood and unloved and I also left feeling frustrated and unappreciated. That is a bombshell!

I had already said that my daughter went into the 'I don't care mode'. I have already shared some details in this respect throughout the book. This conversation throws further light on what I mean. When she kept trying and trying and received no recognitions for her efforts but only criticisms for her mistakes, it became a cycle and I think that over time she could not be bothered to try any longer. However, it was unfortunate that she did not only end up with 'I don't care', she also became anxious and had panic attacks and lost her confidence. A bombshell indeed!

Why am I sharing this with you? I am bringing this to your attention because sometimes you may feel that you are doing okay until someone points it out to you. I will encourage you to listen to your children and your teenagers. Actually listen, without being afraid or offended; actually listen, without interruptions; listen without jumping into conclusions thinking you already know what they are going to say; and actually, listen without thinking of what to say or how to react. I would encourage you to reset your mind to be intentional, learning every day to gain understanding for nurturing your children and teenagers. Sometimes we are so bent on correcting behaviours that we lose sight of what matters: what is causing those behaviours in the first place and the love that we must give to our teenagers regardless of their behaviours; unconditional love. You may feel that your situation is better than mine or that you are quite a positive mother or parent and therefore this may not apply to you. I know that no matter your situation there can always be improvement in one way or another. I also know that if you want to be the best mother and parent that you were purposed to be, knowing the best for your children and supporting them to achieve their best, then I know only of one way that you can achieve this. It is by becoming a committed apprentice and learning from the best.

I am so sorry now for my behaviour and attitude then. I admit I behaved ignorantly because I had no insight and understanding. It is as a result of learning from the best that has brought me to this consideration. Things are different now. I am glad that they are because I am a mother who is committed to being a best mother that she is blessed to be by being a committed apprentice. I would leave these words with you to ponder over:

'Trust in the Lord your God with all your heart, and lean not on your own understanding. In all things acknowledge him, and he shall guide your path.' – Proverbs 3:5-6

Chapter 18

Messages

In this chapter I share a number of general messages that I send to my teenagers and also receive from them. I am sharing this with you because some time ago, I had a mother ask me about the kind of messages I send to my teenagers. So, I thought it would be good to give you examples here in this chapter for your journey. In this way, I know you would be provided with some starting points if you are not sure where to start from or how to go about it. I will also share in this chapter the letter to my daughter and the letter to my son that I shared on Boxing Day in the presence of others. I mentioned these letters in Chapter 12.

I have mentioned previously that I do text my teenagers especially my daughter a lot. This is me using technology where appropriate to nurture my teenagers. That is about it! All I know about and use my phone for, is to make calls, send messages including What's app messages and take photos. Yes, that is me! My son is always teasing me about my phone. According to him my phone is old. Do you know what, yes, it is old, but it still works and functions quite well? For a phone that 'old', like mine, it is actually pretty good. It has a good battery life and what is more, it does exactly what I want it to do perfectly. It is fit for purpose. That is my son and that is my phone!

This day and age, with our children and teenagers glued to their phones, we as parents can also use technology – appropriately to get their attention. I use text messages showing appreciation, recognition, respect and accepting my daughter as a person and my son as a person. I employ the love language, *words of affirmation* to communicate love to my teenagers in my text messages. I must share that I send them messages regardless of whether or not they respond. I do it without expecting anything. It is lovely when they do respond and I appreciate that; however, my focus is not on their response so when it does not happen, I am not offended or disappointed. I do it heartily and unconditionally as to the Lord. I call my daughter Sunflower and my son, LD.

We had been through a lot together as a family; my separation from my husband, that is my children's father, the relationship between my daughter and her father has broken down, they had 'divorced' one another, and my daughter was starting college. There was a lot going on and it got to a time that I could see the emotional strain on my daughter so I suggested therapy and she agreed. So, some time in 2019, my daughter had accessed therapy for about 5 months. And upon review, the therapist suggested that it was important that my daughter was ready and accepted to access therapy not based on the fact that she was doing it to please me; and not because I thought it was good for her. She must recognise the need and want it in order to fully engage in the process. I allowed her to make the decision herself as to whether or not she wanted to continue to access therapy. She chose to discontinue with therapy at the time and this was the text message I sent her:

Me: "Hi Sunflower, I love you so much, no matter what. I just want you to be you and be ok. I thought that you were enjoying therapy and you would continue. But you are the only one who will know whether or not you need help. At the moment you have expressed to me that you do not need help. I accept that. I just want you to know that whenever you would like to access therapy again, I will be here to support you through it. I love you and I am here to support and love you regardless my sunshine sunflower xx. I must say that I am proud of you for giving therapy ago. Well done! Hey by the way your green skirt looked lovely on you."

Daughter: "ty" I suppose it's "thank you."

Implementing a boundary with sensitivity and love with my daughter.

Sometimes when I am required to enforce a boundary, I would explain the situation face to face which I had the opportunity to do on this occasion with my daughter. However, I felt that following it up with a text message for her was appropriate. My daughter did something that resulted in her being grounded and I had to apply the consequence of breaking the boundary empathetically. I put efforts into thinking how to empathise and recognise and appreciate her feelings without succumbing to overlooking the boundary. Empathising with her in the manner that respected her as a person and her feelings would also speak love to her. And although she might not like the boundaries being carried out, she would understand and accept the consequence of her action. This was something that I lacked when I was parenting 'any-how'. But now that I am a committed apprentice under supervision, I am intentional about these things. Implementing boundaries with sensitivity and love for me, is pruning. So here we go:

Me: "Hi Sunflower, I see how you feel sad and angry that your being grounded means you are not able to spend over night with your friend to watch Eurovision. I really empathise with you because I can imagine how much fun you may have together. I also understand that you may feel embarrassed for letting your friend down. However, as your mum, I have to enforce the boundaries and consequences we have agreed together. I love you so much and I would be doing you a disservice if I did not enforce them."

Daughter: "I don't care lol I'm still going."

Me: "I do care. I trust you and I know you will do the right thing."

Appreciation and Recognition and affection

I share with you examples of text messages that I send to my daughter and son expressing appreciation, recognition and affection. By recognising and appreciating their efforts gives them a sense of value and responsibility. It also gives them a sense of purpose for whatever they are doing.

Me: "Hi thank you for doing the vacuuming yesterday. You looked cheerful this morning my sunshine Sunflower. Thank you for sharing with me the fact that you have a boyfriend. You clocked a 'C' in math? Well done. You have no idea how the thought of you brings joy to my heart. I am privileged to be your mother. I am blessed that you are my daughter. God has blessed you my child."

Daughter: She responded with a "photo of her exams result."

Me: "I am glad you passed your exams. God has blessed you. Have a wonderful day. See you later. With imoji kisses on the face."

Me: "Hi LD, you woke up early and sorted yourself out. It is such joy to see that you are taking responsibility for yourself. It is so helpful. I am humbly proud of you. God bless you; I adore you and I love you, kisses imoji."

Me: "Hi LD, thank you so much for your understanding regarding our conversation this morning. Thank you for loving me because I am your mama."

Me: "Hi LD, it was a pleasure helping you with your hair this morning. I really enjoyed it. you are such a handsome young man. I also enjoyed our time together last night as always. I appreciate you for taking your time to do the laundry and making your bed."

My daughter and son were away from home

I send my daughter and my son these messages for them to know that I love them and even though they might not be at home with me, they are in my thoughts. This is reassurance for them to know that I love them regardless of where they are. Sometimes receiving these messages might cheer them up if for instance they are having a bad day. It might just give them a boost of love for the day. Knowing that I am thinking of them in a positive manner speaks love to them. It is not a case of out of sight, out of mind. That is reassuring for anyone including adults and our teenagers too.

Me "Hi my Sunflower and LD. I hope you both had a good night sleep. How are you today and what are you up to today? I am well, just finished church service online, I may have a nap and I have a few things to do with Peace and Love. I will check my website and I will pray. I may watch some movies later too. I love you."

Response from daughter: "love u X."

Me: "Hi Sunflower, how are you today? I hope you had a good night sleep. God bless you. I adore and I love you. Your brother misses you. Have a blessed day."

Me: "Hi LD, I hope you slept well. How did the raid go yesterday? Did you get the Pokémon? I was glad I took you to the spot to join the gym. I love you."

Me: "It's a beautiful day, Sunflower. Have an amazing day. God loves you and I love you.

Me: "Hi LD have a blessed day at school. God loves you and I love you."

Me: "Hi LD and Sunflower, have a blessed day. Do the right thing, be happy be yourself."

Words of recognition and encouragement

Everyone likes to be recognised and encouraged in whatever they do. And guess what our teenagers also want to be recognised and encouraged. It is a way of boosting confidence and giving motivation to our teenagers. I have learned that loving my teenagers in this way will support their foundation and enable them to progress to do their best in whatever purposes God has blessed them with. I have learned to recognise my teenagers' efforts and achievement and encourage them. I do this both face to face and also via text messages. For me, this is a good way of watering my seeds (teenagers). Here are some examples:

Me: "Hi LD, I am humbly proud of you and you should be too. Since we started being intentional about growing our inside, you have made a remarkable progress. I am delighted for you. When I reflect on your experience with your school chef, it is amazing, you have shown wisdom, you have sensitivity to others and communicated well. Well done for all that you do for loving yourself, loving others, being considerate and sacrificing. I am very impressed. Keep it up."

Me: "Hi Sunflower, I am humbly proud of you and you should be too. You did not quit. You went to work in spite of all the issues and I felt how awful you were feeling. But you did not quit Sunflower, you went despite all the anxiousness and the worry. On top of it, your period came and yet you still went. Despite the emotions and the challenges, my Sunflower rose above it and conquered. My sunflower conquered it. watch out anxiety, my sunflower is out to get you. In fact, she has already gotten you anxiety. Well done sunflower, I believe in you."

Me: "Hi Sunflower, how are you doing on your shift? You have got this. Keep your head up and I will see you in the morning. God loves you and I love you."

Me: "Hi LD, I really enjoyed our time this morning. Thank you so much for making your bed and folding your PJs. It was really helpful when I was tidying up the room this morning. I appreciate you. God bless you."

Me: "Hi Sunflower, thank you for the taxi money. It says a lot about you for doing what you agreed and I admire that. Keep it up. I also want to thank you so much for your willingness to swap your book with mine. I really appreciated that. You are kind, thoughtful and I am delighted in you."

Words of affection

I enjoy letting my teenagers know that I love them for them. I love them for being them. This, I believe will fill their emotional love tank. Knowing that you are loved and accepted regardless of whatever, fortifies identity and self-worth. It breeds self-confidence. It supports the emotional foundation that keeps teenagers grounded and enables them to grow the wings to soar. I want that for my teenagers. And as a nurturing mother I use affection to condition the soil.

Me: "Hi LD, I enjoyed you last night. I enjoyed you this morning too. Have a blessed day."

Me: "You are such a handsome young man."

Me: "God loves sunflower and God loves LD."

Response from my daughter: "love you."

Me: "Hi Sunflower, you are in my thoughts, I love you. Have a wonderful day. God bless you"

Daughter: "love you mum XX."

Me: "Hi Sunflower, you are so beautiful and your hair is beautiful. How did I become so privileged to have you as a daughter? God loves you and I love you."

Me: "Hi Sunflower, I was just thinking of you. I love you so much. I just adore you. ☺"

Me: "Hi Sunflower and LD, I am so blessed to be your mother. God loves you and I love you."

Me: "Hi Sunflower, welcome home, it's always good to have you home. Thanks for the compliment at the door, it's refreshing."

Words in the presence of others.

I would say that words in the presence of others is a booster, if you like the manure to foster good yield. It is a way of filling emotional love tanks in a special or quick way. It is a catalyst. I realised the tremendous effect of words in the presence of others when I used it. My teenagers felt valued, appreciated, loved, respected and encouraged. For me, I felt humbled by the fact that loving my teenagers in this manner did not only impact their lives but also everyone present was touched with the tears and love-filled air. The experience was priceless! I was simply fulfilled. Okay, here we go:

Dear LD,

I am delighted in you. I am blessed to be your mother. What a privilege of being your mama. You are growing in humility, under-standing and wisdom. I have watched you grow in self-discipline every day.

You have settled well into waking yourself up using your alarm 'ok google'. I am humbly proud of you because this is so helpful especially in the mornings when we are getting ready for school and work. I watch you empty the recycling bin with admiration. It is such a great help to me when bins have to be collected on Thursday. I appreciate your help. I have observed you settling into turning your phone and TV off at the time that we agreed and making your way to prepare for bed. I enjoy you taking such responsibility and showing discipline. I am delighted in how your attitude towards having your shower and doing work after school has improved.

I love you and I want to serve and help you to develop and grow into the matured man that you are becoming. I do not want to do you a disservice because I love you too much so I would love to teach you and help you to do things for yourself to encourage your independence. I am hoping that the things I teach you would enable you to work together with your future wife and to teach your own children. I love you.

Mama X ☺

PS: You are more than welcome to tell me the things you would like me to teach you.

Dear Sunflower

I am delighted and pleased that you are my daughter. I am such a blessed mother to have you as a daughter. I am grateful for being part of your life. I thank God for your life and the privilege to mother you.

I love and adore you. You are always in my thoughts. I have watched you grow and continue to grow in confidence. Seeing you write your words down before you speak and speaking to people on the phone shows the progress you have made. I have every confidence in you from what I have observed from you these last few months that when you want something, you will go for it without fear. I admire you and I am humbly proud of you. I must say that I am impressed with the growth of your efforts to take care of yourself in terms of personal care. I know that things had been difficult in the past, however I am excited for you that you feel "safe and protected" which is also necessary for your emotional health and wellbeing. I am happy and delighted in you.

Thank you for consenting for me to share my story which also includes you. God bless you, Sunflower.

Madre ☺

I think it is a good way to bring this chapter to an end by saying that:

'Behold, children are a heritage from the Lord, the fruit of the womb is a reward.' – Psalm 127:3

Chapter 19

This is just the Beginning

I had smiles on my face all day. My heart was just filled with joy and I couldn't help but praise God. I went to work in the morning as usual, I dropped off my son and then made my way to work. I worked in a school. Before I left for the school yard and into my little allocated room (I was a nurse for a child in the school), I usually spent a few minutes in my car to drop my daughter a text message. My daughter was sometimes asleep by the time my son and I left home. I had cultivated the habit of purposefully sending her a message in the morning before I started work and if not some point during the day. I had been doing this for years now.

Today, however, I just decided not to send her a message. I did not forget and she was awake when my son and I left home. I just thought that I would give her a break. About 20mins into starting work, that was around 09:21, I was in the process of completing some paper work, when my phone was vibrating indicating a phone call. I took my phone out only to see my daughter's name on my phone. I generally would not answer calls when I was in the classroom, however calls from my children are exception. So, I answered the call and the words that followed were just beautiful.

"Oh sorry," she said, realising from the volume of my voice that I was in the classroom. She continued, "I just called to say that I love you and have a good day... init." My heart just melted, and I felt amazing as a mother. I just felt fulfilled and content. I realised that the perseverance and consistency and the strength of God is paying off. I realised that she actually looked forward to my messages. I just thought to myself that she felt that I could not drop her a message so then she would do it. My God how excellent is your name. To me this screams appreciation, this screams gratitude and this screams that I am doing a good job as a mother. If my children recognise this then I know that my God who gave me the opportunity to steward them is also happy with my progress.

A day prior to this, in the morning my teenagers gave me a review or feedback and I must say that I was pleased with what they said. In fact, I was blessed with what they had to say and my heart was filled with joy, overflowing joy. I realised that God is in control and has brought me this far. I have realised that since I became a committed apprentice and began intentional and purposeful nurturing, my life and my teenagers' lives are different for the better. Our lives are joyful and peaceful. It has been a long journey which is worth every moment of it. I have realised that the consistency and persistency, patience and aiming at doing a good job because God expects that of me with His assistance. By not focusing on my children being grateful for what I do for them; not becoming frustrated because my children's behaviour suggested ungratefulness; and not being afraid of what people might say about my new approach and strategy. I just focus on the fact that I am privileged and have been given the opportunity to be a mother to two wonderful gifts from God. I aimed to do a good job to please Him. I knew that the gratitude would follow in the future when I least expected.

Now, here we are, they are pouring in and the feeling is just priceless. This is fulfilment. It is this fulfilment that I would like every parent like yourselves to experience. I just want to challenge you to review your situation and make your mind up to change certain things in your circumstance to be intentional and purposeful, to be determined to love your children unconditionally in the manner in which Christ loves us. Don't get me wrong it is not easy especially with 'too late syndrome' but it is doable and worthwhile. It is important that we as parents decide to change our perspective away from what the world has taught us or is teaching us and focus on being an apprentice who learns from the best Tutor, the same One who gave us our children. Go to Him and He will show you how to care, nurture and grow them. It is not meant to be this hard. This is not normal, not as intended by the maker. In fact, come to think of it, it was meant to be a two-parent job but looking at our world today we have lots of single mothers doing it on their own. We do also have some single fathers doing it on their own. If it is hard for two parents then it is extra hard for people nurturing by themselves like I find myself. So, we need all the help we can get.

Let talk about the review in a little detail. I asked my son to share his views on me as a mother. I asked him to give me feedback; what he thought of me as a mother, where I can improve. To make it easier for him, I said to him that if he was asked to rate me as a mother from scale of 1 to 10 with 1 being the least and 10 being the best, where would I place? He rated me a 6 for when we were living in our old home as a family of four and he rated me 9 now that we live as a family of three (my son, my daughter and I). According to him, he rated me 6 because, "You used to shout and give harsher punishments – example, standing in the corner. I did not like that at all." But now he rates me a 9 because, "You shout very little, and you give fair discipline. We talk more about good things I have done and when I do something wrong, we always talked about it. We discuss boundaries and their consequences before they are implemented and that is really good. We have lots of fun and we are happy now. You give me lots of hugs and cuddles."

The next day, in the morning, he calls his sister into our bedroom and asks her to give feedback. Their ratings were very similar. She said, "You are a really good mother, now. I rate you 5 for when we lived in our old home and now it's a 9", just as her brother said. She does not talk a lot like my son does. But what she said meant a lot. She shared, "I feel safe and protected now". She added, "I have not been acting rude or misbehaving." I thought this was true because about a couple of weeks before this review, we had a conversation that brought tears to the eyes of the three of us. Since then, I have realised a positive change in her attitude and behaviour. When my daughter shared that she felt 'safe and protected', it made me realise that she had been feeling unsafe and unprotected when we were living in our old home as a family of four. I had no idea about that and this told me that it contributed to making the relationship between her and myself difficult. She lost trust for me as her mother because she felt I did not protect her. Protect her from what and from whom? I have a fair idea but I do not want to jump to conclusions. That is something that I would explore at an appropriate time. You see what God can do when you surrender and look up to him. God is good. My children are my legacy and my treasure. The experience I have shared happened in September 2020.

Growth and Fulfilment

I get it wrong and I stumble from time to time as it is expected of an apprentice. In those moments the Holy Spirit is there to speak with me, pick me up, dust me down and set me straight on the path again. I regain my strength as He strengthens me in my weak moments and encourages me on. It is a journey remember and I get better and better as I grow. And the job satisfaction of being a committed apprentice is invaluable. From peace to joy, to hope, to fulfilment, to meaningful life, to enjoying myself as a person and to enjoying nurturing my teenagers. You name it! From the once tedious job of parenting to the enjoyable stress-free and intentional nurturing of my teenagers.

If you would remember, earlier in this book, I talked about the truth is the truth. Whether we like the truth or not, it does not change. Whether I believe it or not the truth remains the truth. And that settles it! The truth is God created you and I wonderfully and fearfully in His image. God blessed me with my children and he blessed you with yours too. I have chosen to believe the truth and I am encouraging you to do the same. Believe the truth and live the truth, for the truth sets us free. Free from stress, free from hopelessness, free from meaningless life, from wars and battles at home and within my relationships. Free from fear and free from guilt.

He has plans for you as a person and as a mother of your teenagers. He also has plans for your teenagers. It is only when we are in a personal relationship with him that we become enlightened of his plans for us and He teaches us the way to be successful in our purpose here on earth. And the truth is He is the only one that can teach you the way to be successful at nurturing your children and also become successful at supporting them to become successful in their own purposes here on earth – which is also the best for them.

The point I am making here is that, when God employed me as an apprentice of parenthood by blessing me with first my daughter and then my son, I decided to take matters into my own hands when that was not God's plans. So, with no knowledge and experience, I decided I could do this on my own and went my own journey with no guide and support. I was lost and not only that I ended up with an 'alien' in my home, I also ended up with a weak foundation which ultimately crushed us. But I had a wake-up call; a call that I answered; a call that redirected my life. A call that set me straight; a call that has taken me through modules and lessons. A call that led me to peace, joy and hope; a call that enlightened me to the truth I am sharing with you today. A call that has brought blessings to my life; a call that has given me the opportunity to share my story with you. It was a call that I responded to. What do you say? What would your response be? For me, I say:

- This is my truth
- This is my story
- I am a committed apprentice
- I am learning from the Best.
- My journey continues

'Who is wise? Let him understand these things. Who is prudent? Let him know them. For the ways of the Lord are right; the righteous walk in them, but the transgressors stumble in them.' – Hosea 14:9

Prayer

Dear God,

Thank you for the one reading this book.

Thank you for his or her life and situation.

You know what is on their hearts because You are All-knowing God.

Lord Jesus, speak into their lives in a supernatural way.

Enlighten them to Your truth and guide them to Your path in Jesus' Name.

Amen!

Notes

Chapman, G. *The 5 Love Languages of Teenagers: The Secrets to Loving Teens Effectively (Chigaco:Northfield, 2016)*

Moody, V. *The I factor: How Building a Great Relationship with Yourself is the Key to a Happy Successful Life* (Nashville: Nelson Books, 2016)